I0153543

Waifs, Foundlings

and

Half-Orphans

Searching for America's Orphan Train Riders

Mary Ellen Johnson
Founder of the Orphan Train Heritage Society of America, Inc.

HERITAGE BOOKS
2007

HERITAGE BOOKS

AN IMPRINT OF HERITAGE BOOKS, INC.

Books, CDs, and more—Worldwide

For our listing of thousands of titles see our website
at
www.HeritageBooks.com

Published 2007 by
HERITAGE BOOKS, INC.
Publishing Division
65 East Main Street
Westminster, Maryland 21157-5026

Copyright © 2005 Mary Ellen Johnson

All rights reserved. No part of this book may be reproduced or
transmitted in any form or by any means, electronic or mechanical,
including photocopying, recording or by any information storage and
retrieval system without written permission from the author, except for
the inclusion of brief quotations in a review.

International Standard Book Number: 978-1-58549-955-2

Dedication

This book is dedicated to all the Orphan Train Riders I have met in the last 18 years and to those I will meet in the future.

Kay B. Hall went with me to St. Paul, Nebraska in 1987 to attend a function we knew so little about but would change both our lives. This was called a *"New York Foundling Orphans Reunion."* A group of about 60 senior citizens met once a year (first Sunday in May) to catch up on what had happened since the last meeting, a year ago. Often this was the only time they saw each other but they shared a common experience; they all came from the New York Foundling Hospital to find new homes in the west (in this case, Nebraska). Today the gathering is called the *"Nebraska Orphan Train Riders Reunion"* and is still held in the early part of the month of May each year in a different town in Nebraska.

From that day on, we both felt this part of America's history had been sadly neglected and these people were such hardy survivors their stories had to be preserved.

So we went about doing exactly that.

Without the encouragement of friends like Kay B. Hall, Phil Sutton, Charlotte Woodward and my family, I could never have committed myself to this work because it became a passion or obsession, whatever you want to call it, for the next 18 years of my life. I lived for finding new information.

Also, a great deal of credit goes to Annie Azaritti, a producer for Cosgrove-Meurer's, **Unsolved Mysteries** program who came to Arkansas and filmed a segment.

Advanced ages and health problems of survivors prove we need to work even harder to gather their stories and preserve this part of our social history.

One thing I've learned from the Riders is to love life and what it has to offer and to do my best to help someone every day. They are the greatest survivors you will ever meet; a true example for today's foster children.

Mary Ellen Johnson, September 2004

Dedication

This book is dedicated to all the Orphan Train Riders I have met in the last 18 years and to those I will meet in the future. Kay B. Hall went with me to St. Paul, Nebraska, in 1987 to attend a function we knew so little about but would change both our lives. This was called a "Train Ride Reunion." Orphan Train Riders, a group of about 60 senior citizens met once a year (first Sunday in May) to catch up on what has happened since the last meeting a year ago. Often this was the only time they saw each other but they shared a common experience: they all came from the New York Foundling Hospital to find new homes in the west (in this case Nebraska). Today this gathering is called the "Nebraska Orphan Train Riders Reunion," and is still held in the small month of May each year in St. Paul, Nebraska.

Waifs, Foundlings, and Half-Orphans
Searching for America's Orphan Train Riders

Chapter One: ORPHAN TRAIN RIDERS
    Peg's Story   page 1
    Algie's Story   page 3
    Orphan Train Riders Research Center   page 6
Chapter Two: MASS IMMIGRATION; A MAJOR IMPACT
    Changing Life in New York City   page 7
    The Effects on Children   page 11
    Parental Responsibilities   page 12
    Our Cities Charities, No. IV   page 13
    Free-Home-Placing-Out   page 16
        A Study of Events of the Era
Chapter Three: ORPHANAGES AND INSTITUTIONS
    Newsboys Lodging House   page 19
    Sending Children to the Country   page 23
    Children's Aid Society   page 26
    Brace Farm School   page 28
    New York Foundling Asylum   page 31
        The Work of the Sisters of Charity
    History of the New York Foundling Hospital   page 32
        By Alfred G. Vignec
    New York Juvenile Asylum   page 36
    American Female Guardian Society   page 39
    Extracts from the First Report of the First Home
            Industrial School   page 42
    Chicago Orphan Asylum   page 44
    New England Home For Little Wanderers   page 46
    Home for Destitute Catholic Children   page 51
    Jewish Orphanages   page 52
    Traveler's Aid Society   page 55
    Salvation Army   page 55
    Name Change Records in New York   page 56

Chapter Four: RESEARCH AND RESOURCES
    Is There an Orphan Train Rider in My Family?   page 57
    Where Did the Orphans Go?   page 58
    The First Orphan Train Riders   page 58
    Orphan Train Riders   page 62
    Locating Places for the Children   page 63
    Where to Look Next   page 67
    Orphan Train Heritage Society of America   page 70
Chapter Five: REFERENCES and READING LIST
References and Reading List   page 71
Researching an Orphan Train Rider   page 81

INDEX   page 82

List of Illustrations

June 7, 1912 Arkansas newspaper   page 5
Newsboys Lodging House washroom   page 22
Brace Farm School, Valhalla, NY   page 29
CAS Placement card   page 30
Home for the Friendless   page 42
Little Wanderers Advocate Aug. 1908   page 50

Research Tips

Research Tip #1   page 21
Research Tip #2   page 22
Research Tip #3   page 24
Research Tip #4   page 27
Research Tip #5   page 28
Research Tip #6   page 35
Research Tip #7   page 38
Research Tip #8   page 43
Research Tip #9   page 45
Research Tip #10   page 50
Research Tip #11   page 51
Research Tip #12   page 54
Research Tip #13   page 55
Research Tip #14   page 63

Foreword

In August of 1986, an elderly gentleman sat in his living room talking to Mary Ellen Johnson, whom he had just met, about being abandoned as a child in New York City and coming to Arkansas on an "Orphan Train."

"*I hate the Statue of Liberty.*" Algie Braly said with a glimmer of tears coming into his eyes.

He went on to tell how the top of the Statue of Liberty was all he could see from the window in the orphanage dormatory and it was all he could see from the stone enclosed play yard. He felt that it meant being deserted by his mother.

From that day forward, Johnson sought every available scrap of information about these children that she could find. She shared what she learned with anyone interested. Authors such as Andrea Warren, Clark Kidder, Stephen O'Connor, among others, published books in the years following 1986, turning to Johnson for resources.

Cosgrove-Muerer filmed a segment of *Unsolved Mysteries* in 1988 (aired in 1989) using her work. As a result, Sylvia Wemhoff found her brother Joseph Wolk after a separation of 70 years.

The Orphan Train Riders Research Center and Museum she established is the only one in the United States devoted solely to the children who rode the Orphan Trains.

Mary Ellen Johnson and her husband, Leroy, founded, and helped to financially support, the Orphan Train Heritage Society of America, Inc., from 1986 until her retirement in 2004; more than 18 years later.

This book is based upon her work

Acknowledgements

The author is grateful to those who took the time and their talents to write books, newspaper and, magazine articles and to produce videos about the social history of the United States of America.

Peter Holloran's work covering the Boston area is a priceless research tool.

Martin Gottlieb's work about the New York Foundling Hospital certainly fills in details not known previously.

Annette Riley Fry paved the way for this book to be written. Her work is a "must read" for history day competitors.

Marilyn Holt, Andrea Warren, and Holly Littlefield are certainly to be commended.

Jane Peart, Joan Lowery Nixon, and the many, many other fiction authors who have chosen to keep their writings historically accurate have given much reading pleasure to youngsters just learning about the Orphan Train Riders.

There is no way everyone can be listed here but what they have done definitely prove this part of America's history will never be forgotten.

Ben, Ron, Tony, and Renee Johnson encouraged the researching and saving this part of history for future generations as yet unborn even though it took their mother away from time to time and filled her life with purpose other than them and their children.

Last, but not least, I want to acknowledge the man who stood by my side for all these years, Leroy Johnson, telling me I could do this, even if I was just a wife and mother with no formal education except the college of life.

Mary Ellen Johnson

Waifs, Foundlings and Half-Orphans
Introduction

From 1854 until 1929 the emigration of an estimated 200,000 children and poor families took place in America. This 75-year period in America's social history is presently known as the Orphan Trains Era.

The term "orphan" in the early 1850's did not always mean "without any parents." It was recognized as being any child living without adult supervision.

In 1852, New York City had developed a situation with homeless children roaming the streets. Over 10,000 children were estimated to be "orphaned." Living conditions were very severe for most of the population at that time but was especially hard on children of poor families.

Some of these homeless children were actual orphans with both parents deceased. Others were "half-orphans" with one parent living but unable to work or care for the child. A fair number of these "street" children were simply the result of extreme poverty, turned out to fend for themselves.

- **Waifs**– 1) A homeless, neglected wanderer; a stray; 2) Law— Something stolen then abandoned by the thief in his flight to avoid arrest; 3) Anything found and unclaimed; the owner being unknown.

- **Foundling**— 1) A deserted infant of unknown parentage.

- **Half-orphan**-1) A child who has one parent deceased.

Chapter One:
ORPHAN TRAIN RIDERS

Peg's Story

I crawled under the porch so I could hear what the school census taker was saying to my mother.

I guess the school got money for each of us kids who lived in the district. That must have been the reason for her to visit our house and ask questions.

"*Where was Margaret born?*" I heard her ask.

"*New York City.*" My mother replied.

My ears were ringing and I didn't hear the next question. We live in Nebraska. How could I have been born in New York City?

After the school census taker left, I sat for a long time, thinking about what my mother said. I was smart enough to not say anything right away. She would have known I was listening if I'd mentioned it too soon after the visit.

A few days later, I was helping my mother in the kitchen when I asked her when she lived in New York City. She said she had never lived there.

"*Then how come I was born there?*" I asked not really wanting to know but feeling I simply must know or I would burst with curiosity.

"*Margaret, sit down. I need to tell you something.*" She dried her hands that were beginning to tremble.

My head was spinning. Anger swept over me so intense I thought I would die from my heart beating so fast.

"*I am not your child?!!*" I screamed at her. "*Why have you lied to me all these years? Who IS my mother? My whole life has been a lie!*" I let the tears roll down my face as the confusion took over my whole body.

Then she began the story.

Mother and father had a grown son, about 19 years old, but had lost six other children. Elmer was the only one to survive early childhood.

1

They wanted another child, even though they were not young. Mother was 49 and Daddy was 50.

My biological mother, Marie Buckman, placed me in the New York Foundling Hospital when I was three weeks old. She had an older girl with her when she came that day. I assume it was my sister, though I never knew for sure.

My family that took me off the train doted on me and I was very much loved and probably became very spoiled. My father died when I was nine years old. I was very close to him. My mother lived to see my children grown and my brother died a few years after we lost Mother.

I forgave Mother for not telling me the truth earlier in my life. She was so afraid I would want to go back to my true family and not want her to be my Mother. Nothing would have taken me away from her and I believe she finally knew that.

Note: Margaret "Peg" Kildare arrived on an Orphan Train in 1921 from the New York Foundling Hospital in New York City, to Ogallala, Nebraska. Peg's story was published in 1992 in the first of a series of books titled, ORPHAN TRAIN RIDERS; Their Own Stories published by the Orphan Train Heritage Society of America, Inc.

Algie's Story

My real name is Adam Lenard Mischler, and as far as I know; I had three sisters, Madeline, Elizabeth and Barbara. I had two brothers, Johnny and Fred. Fred was the baby.

Our mother put five of us in an orphanage in New York City but she kept the baby, Fred.

I was too young to know who took my sisters and brother. I found out later in my life what happened to them but it was not easy.

The first family that took me treated me very good. They had a big dog that followed me as I walked to school. The dog stopped at the creek I had to cross and in the afternoon, he would be there waiting for me. I love animals and it is probably because of that particular dog.

I was there less than a year when the lady died and I was put into another home.

My second home was with a family (the Guisingers) who had an older daughter. She was especially good to me so I almost had two mothers.

Mr. Guisinger died and once again, I was shipped to yet another home.

This would be my last home because Mr. Braly adopted me seven years after he took me in. He said it was to keep anyone from ever coming to get me away from them.

I had two dogs at the Braly farm. I had to walk three miles to school. But it was not so bad because I walked with the neighbor children.

One evening as I was walking home, I noticed a big black cat lying on a ledge on the side of the mountain. When I got home and told Dad, he knew exactly what it was.

Dad called the neighbors and they came with their dogs and guns. They caught the "cat" which turned out to be a black panther measuring nine feet from the tip of its nose to the tip of its tail.

The two Orphan Train agents, Morgan and Swan, wanted to take me away from the Braly farm because they thought I was not getting to school often enough.

Mr. Braly did not want to give me up. He had a daughter but I was his only son. He talked Morgan and Swan into meeting him in Fayetteville, the county seat. When we got there Dad (Mr. Braly) took me straight to the lawyers office and had adoption papers drawn up right away.

Dad asked me what I wanted my name to be. Since I had never liked "Adam," I changed it to Algier and have been called Algie since then.

I could not have thought any more of my real father than I thought of Mr. Braly. I loved him and he loved me. Mr. Braly's father had been one of the first pioneer preachers to the area. Mr. Braly read the Bible aloud every night. I loved reading the Bible all my life.

I was 15 years old when my father died. I grieved a long time for him. He was about all I had in this world.

Dad Braly had instilled a love of animals in me. He also helped me locate my sisters and brother.

I am thankful that I was given to Mr. Braly at a time in my life when I really needed his kindness and understanding.

Note: Algie's arrival at the Springdale, Arkansas train depot was found in a newspaper article dated June 7, 1912.

Note: To be an Orphan Train Rider, a child would have been born and old enough to travel by 1854. This meant at least five or six years old and possibly no older than 14. However, on this particular trip a 17-month old boy was among the children. Researchers believe he may have left New York City with an older sibling that was taken by the time the train arrived in Springdale, Arkansas.

CHILDREN ALL PLACED

Good Homes Found for Thirteen Homeless Children.

Springdale families who took children in 1912

Quandt, H.

Stokes, J. B.

Joyce, J. A.

Davis, J. L.

Brant, Ed.

Anderson, John

Cline, A. L.

Kelso, W. H.

Church, H. P.

Langridge, J. R.

Moore, J. P.

Homes were found in Springdale and vicinity for thirteen children brought here recently by representatives of the Childrens Aid Society of New York City. J. W. Swan of Clinton, Mo., who accompanied the children here, left latter part of last week for St. Louis, and the two ladies in the party, Miss Anna Lora Hill and Miss Alice Bogardus who accompanied the children on their journey from New York City to Springdale, left Sunday afternoon for Kansas, the former going to Valley Falls, taking with her a little boy who will be placed in a home near that place, he having a brother and sister there. Miss Bogardus went to Marion, Kan., to look after some children placed in homes at that place:

The children brought to Springdale were placed as follows:

Madilene Mischlen, 12 years old, H. Quandt, city.

Elizabeth Mischlen, 11 years old, J. B. Stokes, southwest of town.

Barbara Mischlen, 10 years old, J. A. Joyce, city.

Adam Mischlen, 7 years old, J. L. Davis, Wheeler;

John Mischlen, 5 years old, Ed. Brant, southwest of town.

George Schlesser, 5 years old, John Anderson, city.

Joseph Marr, 17 months old, Rev A. L. Cline, city.

Margaret Lovas, 8 years old, W. H. Kelso, city.

Henry Knuth, 13 years old, Ed. Brant, southwest of town.

Addie Knuth, 11 years old, H. P. Church, northwest of town.

Roy Knuth, 9 years old, J. R. Langridge, Spring Valley

Charles Salverson, 13 years old, Carrie Salverson, 8 years old, J. P. Moore, Springdale.

Orphan Train Riders Research Center and Museum

Mary Ellen Johnson learned about a group of orphans arriving in her home town some 74 years ago while she was working as a publisher's assistant on the **Washington County History Book** project in her hometown of Springdale, Arkansas in August of 1986.

The newspaper article on page 5 of this book caught her attention and curiosity led her to interview survivors.

From the first day she read how the Salverson children had been torn from each others arms and given to different families, but all in the same area, Johnson felt a pull on her "heart-strings" to know more about these children. Years later, the story of the Salverson children, submitted to the history project by Charlotte Woodward would be printed, not only in the history book being compiled but also in the series of books published by the Orphan Train Heritage Society that Johnson founded and paid to have incorporated in 1987.

Algie Braly was the first Orphan Train Rider Johnson actually met and shook hands with. It was one of those life-changing-moments. Johnson and Braly remained close friends until he passed away years later.

It was a number of years into her work before she realized the importance of preserving the life experiences of the Riders. Their traumatic early lives and how they handled the pain and anger has led to setting policies for today's foster children in ways not imagined in 1986 when she began.

One of the most important lessons learned from the Riders has been to NOT separate brothers and sisters, completely. They may have to live in separate households, but they have a right, and deep need, to know about each other.

Teaching children to work has been a strong point with the Riders. Many of them connect self-worth with their work ethic. An orphan's self-esteem is naturally low but need not stay that way as they learn life skills and begin taking control of their destinies.

Chapter Two:
MASS IMMIGRATION; A MAJOR IMPACT

Changing Life in New York City

To understand why so many children were put on Orphan Trains between 1854 and 1929, it is necessary to know what happened in the United States to bring about such a drastic relocation of some 150,000 to 200,000 children and poor families.

Social problems creating the necessity for the Orphan Trains era in America's history were not solely connected to mass immigration but the almost uncontrolled masses entering at the Port of New York certainly strained the economics of the City.

In 1988, National Geographic published a large "coffee table" book titled, **Historical Atlas of the United States.** One section, dealing with immigration, relates by 1775, European settlements in America were divided into diverse ethnic groups. A graph gave the following percentages in 1790:

English	**48.2%**
Black	**19.3%**
Scotch-Irish	**8.5%**
German	**7.2%**
Scottish	**4.3%**
Welsh	**3.5%**
Dutch	**2.5%**
French	**1.7%**
Swedish-Finnish	**0.2%**

At this time, America had less than 3,000,000 residents, according to the World Book Encyclopedia. Six decades (1790-1850) saw not only tremendous growth in population, but also a nation struggling with independence and a fledgling government.

During this same period of time, immigrants arrived at the Port of New York in large numbers. The population of the

United States reached 17 million in 1840. By 1850, population had grown to 23,191,876 with 85% being rural and only 15% considered urban dwellers.

In 1845, the blight of the potato harvest in Ireland had become a famine and in a short six years, over a million people had died of disease and starvation. Nearly a million more came to America, making up 45% of the total immigration in the 1840's.

In 1847, it was estimated that the Irish population in America had reached 105,000, doubling the number arriving in 1846.

A study of living conditions world wide in 1850 shows unrest and poverty many European families were suffering. A chart found in the <u>Germans to America Ships Index</u> by Gilby and Frazier, states from 1850 until 1854, 728,000 immigrants arrived in America. They arrived at the ports of Boston, Philadelphia, Baltimore, New Orleans, Galveston and San Francisco, but the majority arrived at the Port of New York.

Upon arrival, new immigrants found there were not enough jobs, unsanitary housing, language barriers and no extended family to help. Grandparents, aunts and uncles were often left behind in the "old" country.

Some children were orphaned when their parents died at sea as they made the trip. Others were half-orphans when their mothers died in childbirth often leaving behind nearly a dozen other children. Many fathers were seamen who were away from home and could not care for the remaining children. The older ones simply took care of the younger ones, when they could.

Job safety was not an important issue in the early 1850's. When a father was injured beyond being able to work, the family often went hungry. There were not a lot of jobs for women.

History has documented the importance of immigrant labor to build America. One such documentation does involve women.

Cotton mills in Lowell, Massachusetts, advertised for much needed female laborers in the 1840's. They recruited women immigrants to recruit French Canadians by holding interviews in towns such as Rouses Point, New York. Dormitories housed the women workers.

As the new nation emerged, problems mounted.

The federal government struggled to settle issues of slavery which was reaching the crisis point as the immigrants arrived.

America was also still dealing with internal population problems between descendants of early European settlers and Native American Indians.

Between 1830-1840, some 70,000 Native Americans were removed from their homes in the southeast. Over 16,000 traveled, mostly on foot, to the Territory of Oklahoma, along the notorious Trail of Tears. Along the way, over 4,000 died.

Unrest continued as the nation kept growing.

In 1837, newspaper man, Rev. Elijah Lovejoy was shot to death by a mob while trying to safeguard the press on which he published his weekly anti-slavery paper. He had already lost three presses since moving the previous year from the slave state of Missouri, where he edited the **St. Louis Observer.**

In 1838, Pennsylvania Hall, site of anti-slavery meetings, was burned to the ground by a mob who feared losing their jobs if the slaves were freed.

Texas became a state in 1845, a "slave state."

By 1847 Frederick Douglass was publishing his newspaper, **The North Star**, in Rochester, New York, and in 1849 was speaking out on the "*horror of trafficking in the souls and bodies of men,*" making him one of the best known black abolitionists of his age and such a celebrity that a song was written about his life.

Ethnic groups continuing to arrive at the Port of New York, gravitated to live near their own countrymen in order to understand the language and communicate. New York

City became a series of ethnic neighborhoods tied by the thread of city government.

Irish Catholics and the Jewish population received harsh treatments many times because of their religious beliefs.

The "Draft Riots" of 1863 brought even more turmoil to inhabitants of the fast growing City.

> *July 1863, Draft Riots left more than 100 people dead in the streets of New York City. Mobs of Irish immigrants tore up railroad tracks, ransacked shops, and burned an orphanage for black children. Looting continued until the police were reinforced by troops fresh from the victory at Gettysburg.*

In researching the history of a section of New York City known as the Five Points, **Valentine's Manual of Old New York 1855** contained artist's conception of the slums and squalor in the area of Orange Street (now Baxter); Cross Street (now Park) and Anthony Street (now Worth) in lower Manhattan.

Public unrest, political immorality, chaos and non-regulatory laws governing housing, sanitation and social injustices created a very unhealthy environment for families. Children were especially affected as they were turned out to work as young as six years old. There were no labor laws protecting children from hard and dangerous labor.

*Note: In 2003, the Draft Riots became the topic of a movie titled, **"Gangs of New York."**

The Effects on Children

During this period in history children had no rights. Children were a possession that could be taught to work and help support the family.

In Ronald G. Walters' book, "**American Reformers 1815-1860**" published in 1978, he makes the following statement:

"As reformers learned more about dependent classes, they came to see differences and to realize that even the best of almshouses and prisons were not beneficial for every sort of inmate. The insane and children, in particular, had a rough time when thrown in with seasoned paupers and rogues. Concerned men and women began to consider what sort of treatment might be more appropriate for them. The answer was new, special asylums. Just as some reformers' interests clustered around antislavery, pacifism, and women's rights, the commitments of others focused on almshouses and prisons, and then broadened to include more novel institutions.

The first facility for juvenile delinquents, the New York House of Refuge, opened its doors to wayward boys and girls on New Year's Day 1825."

Boston's House of Refuge was built in 1826 and Philadelphia's came in 1828. By the late 1850's they appeared in cities as widely scattered as New Orleans, Chicago and Providence. In 1848 Massachusetts opened the first state-supported reform school; followed by New York in 1849.

As early as 1832, with the founding of the Boston Asylum and Farm School for Boys, philanthropists began to reach out for the idle and rowdy minors who, if not helped, were likely candidates for the Houses. Of most consequence were the New York City labors of Charles Loring Brace, a former divinity student and ex-assistant to an urban missionary. His Children's Aid Society (1853) was an inspiration to public and private charities across the land. Having as its purpose elimination of pauperism and criminality, it was a well-diversified enterprise providing everything from education to lodging for city children--all the while being run on 'scientific principles' and teaching self-reliance, hard work, and thrift.

Parental Responsibilities

Jobs for women were scarce at best. Some were able to work in the garment industry as the modern industrial age evolved but factory fires often killed women workers trapped on upper floors.

One such incident printed in the newspapers, stated the women's legs were chained to their machines to prevent them from taking too many "breaks." The supervisor had the keys on his pocket. When the fire broke out the women were trapped. During the *Triangle Shirtwaist Factory Fire*, 124 women were killed. One can only imagine the number of children left motherless as a result of such disasters.

Homeless, children without adult supervision, lived on the streets of New York City in large numbers. In 1852, the Chief of Police estimated 10,000 homeless children were living in New York City.

At night, children lay down to sleep where they could find warmth and some amount of security. They lay under steps, in barrels, under bridges, on the docks under protective coverings, or in doorways. Jacob Riis documented these children in photographs he took as a police reporter.

Annette Riley Fry authored **The Orphan Trains** in a series, **American Events**, published by New Discovery books; Macmillan Publishing Company, in 1994. In this book, Fry describes diseases that took their toll on families living in overcrowded, unsanitary slums. Tuberculosis was always present. Epidemics of cholera, yellow fever, and typhus thrived leaving many children orphaned.

Alcoholism led to abuse and disruption of family life and again, the children were neglected or conditions were so bad they simply ran away to live in the streets.

It is hard to imagine how these little human beings managed to survive the cruelties life thrust upon them, but many did and went on to lead decent lives; at least those who talked about it seemed to have had the better sort of life.

Our Cities Charities, No. IV
(Reprinted from original text)

Prior to the year of grace 1848, the attention of the benevolent and philanthropic citizens of New York does not seem to have been particularly called to the condition of the neglected vagrant and homeless children of the City. The House of Refuge was, indeed, performing its beneficent work for the juvenile delinquents; orphans and half-orphan asylums garnered up those who were deprived of a parent's care, and were brought under their notice; the Randall's Island Nursery, and the Home for the Friendless, took charge of many of those who were utterly dependent and helpless; but there were very few who were not startled, when told in the report of Mr. G. W. Matsall, Chief of Police for the year 1848-9, that there were nearly 10,000 children in the City not reached by any of these institutions, who never attended the Public Schools, but who lived upon the streets, many of them having no other home, night or day. They were not criminals in the eye of the law, for their thefts, if they were guilty of stealing, were of very small amounts, and almost entirely food or fuel to keep them from perishing. Some of them gained a precarious subsistence for themselves or their parents by pilfering and begging; others swept the crossings, picked over the ash-boxes, gathered rags, bones and refuse paper; others still sold matches, tooth-picks, or other small articles, or peddled apples, oranges and flowers; a large class were newsboys, and print and ballad sellers; others were organ-grinders, statuette-sellers, or renders of Bohemian and Dresden ware.

Many of them slept in alleys, boxes, old wagons, or on the pavement over the printing vaults, where the heat would impart some warmth to their half-clad and chilled limbs, in then winter, and in summer laid them down upon the benches or grass of the Park. All were miserably clad, and many of them half-starved. From three-fourths to four-fifths of them were of foreign parentage, and in many cases were compelled, by their unnatural parents, to supply them, from their scanty gains with the means of intoxication.

The statistics of Mr. Matsell's report were at first regarded as exaggerations, but the visitors of the associations for the Improvement of the Condition of the Poor, who had the opportunity of thorough investigations, fully confirmed them, and, indeed, demonstrated that they did not completely represent the magnitude of the evil.

The first effort made to reach these neglected children, which has come to our knowledge, was the establishment of a Boys' Meeting, by members of the Carmine Street Presbyterian Church and others in 1848, at first in a hall at the corner of Christopher and Hudson streets, and subsequently in Amos street. Those who entered upon this enterprise had found that these ill-clad, unwashed, unkempt children

13

could not be drawn into any of the existing Sabbath Schools, or churches. Rough as they were, they were unwilling to go among those who were better clad than they, and the only way of reaching them was to establish meetings for them alone, and by means of familiar conversation and lecturing, by singing pleasant and lively songs of a religious and moral character, by pictures, maps, illustrations, and by anecdotes and simple instruction, to endeavor to improve their hearts. At first, the effort seemed likely to prove a failure, those little street Arabs, wild and restless as an untamed colt, could not be kept still, or brought into a condition of subordinations; many times it was found necessary to call in the aid of the Police to preserve order, but at length the children began to feel that it was a shame to treat with rudeness and violence those who only sought to do them good, and in their rough way they became civil and comparatively quiet.

The succeeding year a second Boys' Meeting was established in Wooster-street, through the unwearied efforts of Mrs. George B. Cheever, and the knowledge that was there acquired of the habits and needs of these poor children, stimulated those who had become interested in their condition to try to do something more for them. They came with tolerable regularity, indeed, to the Boys' Meetings, but any good impressions which might have been made there, were speedily effaced amid the profanity and obscenity of their associates and the wretchedness of their homes, if such places as they dwelt in could be called homes. Many of them who were willing to work could find no work to do, and with the two great prompters to evil — hunger, and idleness — constantly at hand, they could not easily be restrained from falling into vice.

The Juvenile Asylum and the Five Points House of Industry were started about this time, and some of these wayward and neglected children were gathered into both, but in several quarters of the City they still swarmed in crowds, and the faithful workers, whose hearts were pained by their conditions, felt that something more must be done for them, or they would swell, to a fearful extent, the army of crime. Honest labor and removal from evil and corrupting influence, were as much a necessity to them as to the poor girls, to whom Mr. Pease acted the part of an angel of mercy. Where the disposition to do good exists, there is usually combined with it a fertile invention which readily finds the way and means of doing it.

It was so in this case. The opportunity of acquiring a livelihood by honest toil was felt to be a first necessity. For this purpose those most active in the Boys' Meetings having organized themselves, in February, 1853, as the "Children's Aid Society," and appointed a Board of Trustees of different denominations Hon. John L. Mason being Chairman, Rev. C. L. Brace, already know as a brilliant writer and conversant with European reformatory efforts, as Secretary and J.E. Williams, Esq., of the Metropolitan Bank, as Treasurer, commenced operations. A workshop for pegging shoes was opened, and as many of the boys as could be induced to work employed in it. From thirty to forty boys daily worked in this shop, earning from $1.25

to $ 4 per week. In all 115 boys were furnished with work during the first year, many of whom after a time were sent to good places in the country. Owing to some adverse circumstances the shop did not pay its way, but fell in debt the first year nearly $200.

Industrial Schools were next established for girls where they might be instructed in books half the day and taught sewing or some light trade the other half, being furnished with a plain, cheap dinner, and sometimes with two meals a day, and clothed with the garments which they themselves assisted in making, A paid matron presided over these schools, assisted by volunteer teachers, mostly from the wealthier classes, who, with a zeal, earnestness and perseverance worthy of all praise, engaged in duties which required no ordinary amount of patience, courage and fortitude, Two of these schools were established the first year—one in Roosevelt street, afterwards removed to Oliver, and subsequently to Cherry-street, and the other in Houston-street.

It was still felt that unless these children could be removed from the associations by which they were surrounded, — the squalor and filth, obscenity and blasphemy, and that utter disregard of the decencies of life, which marks so many of the huge tenement houses where the abject poor do mostly congregate—there was but little hope of their growing up virtuous and pure in character. Homes must be found for them in the country. To accomplish this, circulars were address to clergymen, respectable farmers, manufactures and mechanics in the neighboring States, soliciting applications from them for boys and girls to be employed on farms, in work-shops and manufactories in the country. Responses were received offering employment for 300 children, and 207 were sent to places, of which 20 were taken from the prisons, where they had been committed as homeless vagrants. Most of these children did well, and under their changed circumstances gave evidence that they were attempting to lead a new and better life.
[Reprinted from the original text in the New York Times]

Jacob A. Riis, a police reporter and photographer, turned social reformer, fought for the elimination of slum conditions in New York's Lower East Side. His first published book was titled **How The Other Half Lives.** Riis came to America from Denmark when he was 21 years old (1870). At this time, a depression was deepening and he experienced the joblessness, hunger and homelessness suffered by other immigrants.

Free-Home-Placing-Out
A Study of Events of the Era

Charles Loring Brace had a genuine compassion for children and felt deep within his heart that a home in the country would be better for the child than to remain in the City with all of the immoral temptations surrounding them. The solution seemed clear to the young minister.

A visionary with a very unrealistic view of the true hardships of life in rural America, Brace saw only the advantages a child would have if he or she could be taught good morals and a strong work ethic. For some it worked. Others became little more than servants who were given small amounts of food, unhealthy shelter, scant clothing and limited schooling at best.

The revolutionary method of caring for America's foster children, **"free-home-placing-out"**, had been going on for 22 years before the first train ran from New York to San Francisco in 1876. Until that time, children had traveled on boats, trains and horse-drawn wagons from the institutions in Boston and New York City to the "west" in hopes of finding a new home.

A number of events took place in 1853, the year Charles Loring Brace and a group of prominent businessmen formed the New York Children's Aid Society in an effort to keep children off the streets of the City.

In 1853 the first step was taken toward the consolidation of seven separate railroads between Albany and Troy on the east, and Buffalo and Niagara Falls on the west, into the New York Central Railroad.

This same year a World's Fair was held in New York at the Crystal Palace, on the site of Bryant Park. Sadly, only five years later, the Crystal Palace burned to the ground.

The next year, 1854, Fernando Wood was elected mayor and the Packer Institute for Girls was founded in Brooklyn. A group of 46 children of "workable age" were sent out of New York City to Dowagiac, Michigan, in an experimental plan placing children from the City into farm families where they would have an opportunity to learn a good solid work ethic.

Then came the War Between the States.

For a period of six months, the Union forces commandeered the trains and no children were sent "west."

Over 1,200 people were killed during the "Draft Riots" in 1863. Mothers were left with small children and no way to earn a living.

Mourners lined the streets of New York City in 1865 as the funeral cortege of Abraham Lincoln moved through the City taking the President to Springfield, Illinois for burial.

Four years later, 1869, the panic of "Black Friday" occurred as a result of an attempt to corner the gold market on the New York Stock Exchange.

Men had jobs. The first Grand Central Terminal opened for business at 42nd Street in 1871 but in 1872, over 40,000 men were idle as a result of a general strike of all building industries. Families suffered. No money coming in meant there was little or no food or sanitary housing families could afford on limited income. Children were taken to orphanages to be fed and clothed.

The City was growing at such a rapid pace that a group of young men met at the home of Theodore Roosevelt to form the "City Reform Club."

When the Statue of Liberty was unveiled in 1885, children had been riding "orphan trains" out of New York City for 31 years.

More disastrous living conditions hit families in 1888 when the "Great Blizzard" dropped 22 inches of snow over New York and raged for three days. Many died.

Building once again picked up in the City as Carnegie Hall and a second Madison Square Garden was constructed.

As a prelude to mass immigration to America, Ellis Island opened in 1892.

In 1896, the Greater New York Bill was passed by the state legislature, annexing Manhattan and the Bronx comprising the boroughs of Richmond, Brooklyn and Queens. A commission was appointed to draw up a new charter for the new city.

The same year the Stock Exchange Building at Broad and Wall Streets was completed, New York City witnessed the breaking of all immigration records when some 857,046 foreigners arrived, 1903.

The Panama Canal opened in 1914 and permanent lighting was placed in the Statue of Liberty in 1916 but the United States declared war on Germany in 1917 and New York became the chief port of embarkation for the American Expeditionary Forces.

An epidemic of influenza swept the City in 1918 killing many women and children along with their husbands and fathers. Another disaster occurred in 1920 when a bomb exploded at the corner of Wall Street and Broad Street killing 33 persons and injuring over 300.

Night airmail was established between New York and Chicago in 1925 followed by the first telephone conversation between New York and London in 1926, and Lindbergh's celebrated return to New York from his solo flight to Paris in 1927.

As New Yorkers broke ground for the Museum of the City of New York and the Graf Zeppelin made its second arrival during a record-making round-the-world flight, tensions were mounting following years of speculation as the New York Stock Exchange, and other markets, were swept by what is called a "psychological panic." Billions of dollars in market values disappeared in a few days. Today is it known as the *"crash of the stock market."*

It was 1929. The year the Orphan Trains quietly ended and the history of 75 years of social development in the foster care sector came to an end.

Chapter Three:
ORPHANAGES AND INSTITUTIONS

The Newsboys Lodging House

In 1854 the "Newsboys' Lodging House" was opened in the Sun Buildings, corner of Fulton and Nassau streets, under the charge of Mr. C. C. Tracy. These boys were found to constitute a community by themselves,' governed by certain simple laws, most rigorously executed, but owing little allegiance to any other code, civil or moral. Very few of them had any homes, their lodging-places being in the streets, boxes, alleys, or entries to the printing offices or in summer in the Park. They were very ragged and dirty, but usually shrewd, intelligent, and keen at shifting for themselves and making a bargain. The earnings of many of them were quite large, but were almost invariably squandered in attendance upon theaters or gambling. They were regarded by those who knew them best as the hardest and most uncontrollable of all the street children of the City.

The officers of the Society had made a wise selection of the man for Superintendent of this department of their labors, Mr. Tracy was, perhaps, better qualified for the work than any man they could have found. Cool, calm, collected, an utter stranger to fear, he yet had in large measure that electic sympathy for boys, and such boys as were to come under his care, which insured his finding his way speedily to their hearts. We half suspect that he was a wild boy himself, he is so thoroughly versed in boy-nature. Added to this sympathetic head, he possessed much mechanical ingenuity, and great fertility is expedient for interesting and influencing these restless, untamed boy-men, whose experiences of hardship and suffering had made them old even in childhood.

Mr. Tracy entered upon his work amid many discouragements. The lodgings were to be let to the boy at 6 cents a night, but a condition of administrations was, that the applicant should first submit to a bath; this, to the boys whose skins had had no acquaintance with water often for months, was at first an exceedingly distasteful requirement. Free dirt had hitherto been one of the most highly-prized privileges, and it was not without a struggle that they abandoned it. After a few ablutions, however, the bath-tub became a decidedly popular institution. The next great difficulty was to keep the lads in order, or to arrange them into classes for the evening school. For some time the spirit of insubordinations was so rife, that any man of less faith and patience than Mr. T. would have given up in despair; but at length there began to be some evident improvement. The boys were cleaner, quieter and more respectful, and the obscene and profane language, which had at first been the staple of their conversation, was abandoned, at least in the lodging-house.

Mr. Tracy attended to their bodily aliments and injuries (not few in their rough-and-tumble life,) he helped them occasionally when unlucky and in danger of "punching" from bullies; and while he sometimes engaged with them in their boisterous play, brought constantly to bear upon them the highest and purest votives. This was done without cant or ostentations, and it began ere long to produce a salutary effect. To encourage economy among them, he contrived a table with apertures in the top, each connecting with a little box having the boy's number on it in the drawer, into which he could drop every night a portion of his daily earnings, and persuaded the boys to keep the "bank," as they called the table, closed for two months, At the end of that time it was opened, and the boys were astonished at the amount of savings they had accumulated, Most of the money was expended for winter clothing, and many of the little ragamuffins were better clothed than ever before in their lives. To check their tendency to gambling, Mr. Tracy introduced the game of draughts, and some of the boys were fond of reading, he established a reading-room and library for their benefit. The lodging-house is still maintained, and now affords a shelter for some of the other street-boys as well as the newsboys. The evening school is kept up, and is useful in furnishing the rudiments of education to children who would otherwise have no opportunity of acquiring them. Supper is now furnished to such of them as have four cents to pay for it, and they have a free dinner and an hour of religions instruction of Sunday. The boys have each a drawer, or rather a large pigeon-hole, with a door which locks, where they deposit their best clothes, (rags being a necessary uniform for the newsboy,) and on Sundays and grand occasions, many of them appear well dressed.

At the end of each month the "bank" is opened, and such of the saving of each boys as he does not draw for clothing or other expenses, are deposited to his credit in the Sixpenny Savings Bank. Many of them after having accumulated a sum sufficient to start them fairly, either find a situation in the country or as apprentices in some good trade, or occasionally establish a little shop on their own account. Three years since, Mr. Tracy resigned as Superintendent of the Lodging-house, to take charge of another department of the work of the Society, the conducting of companies of children to the West — since that time it has had, we believe, three Superintendents. It is at present in charge of Mr. C. O'Conner, formerly one of the Society's Visitors, and under his care it maintains its previous efficiency; from 70 to 80 boys nightly find lodgings there, and in its pleasant rooms are attracted away from the pernicious influences which formerly led them astray. He who shall visit the Newsboy's Lodging-house, expecting to see models of quietness and good behavior; boys who would be patterns of correct deportment for school-teachers or Sunday-school superintendents to parade before visitors, will be grievously disappointed; but he who can discern, under a rough and perhaps blunt and uncouth demeanor, the virtues of frankness, generosity, independence and self-reliance, coupled perhaps with some recklessness and swagger, and occasionally a little sauciness,, will conclude, after careful observation, that many a boy brought up to the possession of wealth and luxury, and offered every advantage of education, does not play his part in the world so well as some of these poor newsboys.

In describing thus fully the home provided for the little new-vendors, we have digressed from our historical narrative of the other operations of the Society. In 1855, the Industrial Schools for girls had increased to four, and

20

two others were placed under the supervision of the Society. These Schools numbered 850 girls, of whom full four-fifths were of foreign parentage. Many of these, under the instructions there received, and their subsequent locations in Christian families through the exertions of their teachers and the officers of the Society were saved from an impending life of shame and, in their new homes, grew up to unsullied womanhood.

The boy's meetings had increased in numbers, and their good results had led other persons, not connected with the Society to establish similar meetings in other parts of the City. At the beginning of 1855 ten of these meetings were in existence, with an average attendance of over 1,000 boys. Near the close of the year an Italian School was established for the little organ-grinders, statuette sellers and rag-pickers of the City, in a room kindly furnished by the Fire Points House of Industry. The school was held from 5 1/2 to 8 o'clock P.M., and was attended by from 70 to 80 children, mostly of Italian birth or descent. They were taught by a countryman of their own, Mr. Cesqua. The School is still continued, and is prosperous, its numbers having increased to 90 children in regular attendance but the little organ-grinders have generally ceased to come. [End of reprint.]

Today most of the surviving ledgers kept by former residents of the Newsboys Lodging House are carefully guarded by the Children's Aid Society in New York City.

The ledgers tell a story, in themselves, of the boys who were there and something about their managerial abilities. The Children's Aid Society is proud of the acts of kindness that gave these boys a chance at life. Many boys wrote letters thanking the caretakers at the Children's Aid Society for giving them an opportunity to make a life for themselves with families of their own. Several of such letters have been reprinted in Annual Reports published by the Society.

RESEARCH TIP # 1:

If you believe the person you are researching may have lived at the Newsboy's Lodging House, contact the Children's Aid Society for verification.
Children's Aid Society – Archivist
Lord Memorial Building
150 East 45th St.
New York, NY 10017

THE WASH-ROOM IN THE NEWS BOYS' LODGING HOUSE JUST BEFORE SUPPER TIME.

Sketches, such as this one, appear in the annual reports of the Children's Aid Society beginning in 1853.

RESEARCH TIP #2:

The Internet is an excellent source for finding old books. Sources such as Amazon.com, E-bay, etc., often turn up books long out of print. Some towns are fortunate enough to have a book store that sells old books and the owner will be a valuable resource. Several books have been written about the Newsboys' Lodging House.

Sending Children to the Country
(Excerpts from Annual Reports of the Children's Aid Society)

The operations of the Society in relocating children in the country, were greatly increased during the year 1855, with 800 children and 63 adults having been provided with places, nearly all of them in the Eastern and Middle States. Its gross receipts were about $10,000.

In 1856 the same general policy was pursued as in the preceding year. A Children's Aid Society was established in Brooklyn through the efforts of some of the visitors of the New York Society. This year there was an increasing demand for children, from some of the Western States, and 192 were sent to Michigan, Illinois, Iowa and Wisconsin.

The year 1857 was, in some respects, a new era in the history of the Society. The financial pressure which occurred in the autumn of that year fully tasked its energies and resources. Its income was much greater than in any previous year, and the calls upon its liberality, both in supplying the necessities of its industrial schools and lodging houses, (it has this time, and has still, a girls' lodging-house as well as one for the boys,) and in aiding in removing to the West children and adults, were increasing.

We learn from its fifth report that 943 persons were, during this year, provided with places, of whom 275 were adults, principally sewing and trades girls, and 328 of the whole number were sent to the West, mostly to Michigan, Indiana, Illinois and Iowa.

Other societies, some of them impoverished for the season, sent companies of children and adults to the same States. The motives which prompted these efforts to remove adults to a distance from the City, where they might obtain employment, were noble and philanthropic, and precautions, supposed to be sufficient were taken to prevent those of vicious and disreputable character from being enrolled in the companies; but the event proved that, in a very considerable number of cases, (a small portion of the whole, doubtless, yet sufficient to give much occasion for regret and reproach,) persons were sent out whose subsequent conduct affixed an odium upon all the succeeding efforts of those under whose charge they came. The Children's Aid Society, there is reason to believe, was more cautious than some of the others in regard to the character of its protégés but some of these turned out badly, and, being the best known by name, it was compelled to bear much of the blame which did not justly belong to it. Children sent out by all the Societies did much better than the adults. The home policy at the Society, in 1858, was similar to that of preceding years. Its plan of sending children to the West had, in the view of its messengers, proved so successful the preceding year, that it was materially amplified in this, though they were located in somewhat different sections; Indiana taking the lead, and Ohio and Illinois following, where Michigan and Iowa received very few. Over 500 children were sent to the west during the year.

"During the year just closed (1859) 814 children and adults have been located, about one half at the west; of whom 222 were taken from the Randall's Island Nursery; 352 of the whole number have been sent to Illinois and a few to Ohio and Michigan. A large number of children are reported as connected with the Industrial Schools under the supervision of the Society. The receipts were not far from $12,500. The Society employs four visitors to visit the homes of the poor, as well as the children in the Industrial Schools, and when they are deemed proper subjects for emigration, bring them to the Society's rooms for further examination.

In a previous article of this series, we have alluded to the diverse views entertained on this subject of the deportation of children to the West by the managers of the two Societies most largely engaged in it, and have given, with considerable detail, the plan adopted by the Juvenile Asylum, and the reasons argued by them for it. It remains for us to present the plan adopted by the Children's Aid Society"

(Written in early 1859.)

A few orphanages and poor houses existed in New York City in 1850 but even in the best of circumstances, living conditions were not good.

Some states were making an effort to solve their social problems.

By 1827, Massachusetts had passed a law requiring every town of a population of 500 or more families to have a high school. A year later the Workingman's Party organized and part of its platform was advocating social reform and free education.

Various societies were formed to "cure the social ills" of the times.

RESEARCH TIP #3:

Reg Niles' authored " Adoption Agencies, Orphanages and Maternity Homes," ISBN 0-9604200-1-0, a good reference for histories of these agencies, orphanages, asylums and maternity homes. He is recognized as an authority on the subject. Today, much information can be taken from the Internet, but the Niles book is still considered true documentation as he gives the information first by states, then by cities within that state.

Some records of the New York Infant Asylum, which merged with the New York Nursery & Child's Hospital in 1910, can be located through:
New York Hospital Cornell Medical Center/Archives
1300 York Ave.
New York, NY 10021

Records of the New York Child's Foster Home Services, Sheltering Arms and Speedwell may be obtained by writing to:
Sheltering Arms Archives
122 East 29th St.
New York, NY 10016

Records of the Brooklyn Nursery and Infants Hospital at one time were available through the Salvation Army – Foster Home & Adoption Services in New York City.

The Orphan Asylum Society of the City of Brooklyn's records may be accessed through:
Brookwood Child Care
363 Adelphi St.
Brooklyn, NY 11238

In 2003, lists of children received by the New York Juvenile Asylum became available on the Internet.

A number of websites on the Internet contain valuable research materials on various orphanages and almshouses. Check for accurate mailing addresses before contacting the above resources as storage of archived records change in time. Ellis Island has lists available on the Internet. Sometimes there is a small charge for services. Even with the charges, the cost is much less than traveling and researching in person.

Check out Orphan Train Heritage Society's website at:
http://www.orphantrainriders.com

Children's Aid Society

A young minister, Charles Loring Brace, born in Litchfield, Connecticut, June 19, 1826, was on the brink of changing social history when he returned to New York City from an extensive trip to Europe in 1852. But nothing in the life of this 26-year old, upper middle-class minister gave him a clue as to the vast numbers of lives he was about to affect.

Young Brace, educated to become a city pastor, walked the streets of New York City looking into the faces of homeless children without much hope for a better life. Soon he began to feel his work could be of more benefit if he served as a city missionary.

Years later, Emma Brace, in 1894, wrote of her father's work beginning with an association between himself and Rev. Mr. Pease at the Five Points, with an occasional visit to Blackwell's Island.

Brace wrote the following to his father, "*I don't care a straw for a city pastor's place. I want to raise up the outcast and homeless, to go down among those who have no friend or helper, and do something for them of what Christ has done for me.*"

Emma Brace went on to write that in a few months he became convinced that the effort to reform adults was 'well-nigh' hopeless so he turned his attention to the children he might help.

The result was organizing "boys meetings" to be held on Sunday evenings and designed to draw the roughest class of loafers from about the docks, and to reach and influence them by stories and allegories.

The aim was to bring about moral reform that would lead the boys to achieve good and honest lives for themselves. At a time when orphan asylums, almshouses and pest houses were the only "social services" the idea of an organization devoted to children was revolutionary.

Emma Brace writes, "*What soon struck all engaged in these labors was the immense number of boys and girls floating and*

26

drifting about our streets, with hardly any assignable home or occupation, who continually swelled the multitude of criminals, prostitutes, and vagrants....It was clear that whatever was done, must be done in the source and origin of the evil---in prevention, not cure."

Several gentlemen in various sections of New York City had been trying to better conditions for young boys and girls for some time. Their efforts were falling short of the dire need. On January 9, 1853, they asked C. L. Brace to head up this new "mission to the children."

For doing this, he would be paid $1,000 a year.

Brace wrote to his father, *"I have hesitated a great deal, as it interrupts my regular study and training, but this is a new and very important enterprise. The duties are to organize a system of boys' meetings, vagrant schools, etc., which shall reach the whole city; to communicate with press and clergy; to draw in boys, find them places in the country, get them to schools, help them to help themselves; to write and preach, etc., etc."*

In March of 1853, a circular was printed naming the new association as the Children's Aid Society.

A key phrase in his statement, **"find them places in country"** would lead, within a little over one year, to the first group of children participating in what we, today, call the 'orphan trains era' in America's history.

RESEARCH TIP # 4:

Miriam Z. Langsam wrote *Children West*, in 1964, published by the University of Wisconsin Press, which contains the history and purposes of the Children's Aid Society. In her work, she has four tables detailing ethnic origins of placements; family status of placements 1873 & 1897; yearly placement figures 1853-1890 and a comparison of placements in relation to population. Langsam's work is considered a "must read" for researchers. Langsam also appeared in the PBS documentary, Orphan Trains produced for American Experience by Janet Graham and Edward Gray.

Brace Farm School

In preparation for placing out on farms in the Midwest, children were sometimes taken out of the City to Kenisco Station in Westchester County, New York, to the Brace Farm School to live and work for a time.

Surviving records of the Brace Farm School are under the control of the Children's Aid Society.

In 1912, Maurice de Leleu was placed in the Brace Farm School at Valhalla, New York. He rode an Orphan train to Weatherford, Texas, in October of the same year. In his later years, he visited the site of the Brace Farm School with his adult children where he walked on the grounds and talked about being happy while there. He would have been about 13 years old at the time he lived at the Brace Farm School.

In 1986, when several Orphan Train Riders met at a Reunion, they spoke lovingly of the Brace Farm School and several descendants of Riders who had passed away stated that some of the best memories their ancestor had was of being there.

The Brace Farm School was visited numerous times by President Franklin Roosevelt and his mother. The Orphan Train Riders Research Center and Museum has on display a photograph of the President and his mother sitting in an open top touring car surrounded by children living at the Brace Farm School.

Today all signs of the Brace Farm School have been removed in the name of progress but the good that was done there goes on from generation to generation. Children were taught a good work ethic and how to have good relationships with each other.

RESEARCH TIP # 5:

Maurice's story can be found on page 247 of the book, ORPHAN TRAIN RIDERS; Their Own Stories Vol. 1 published in 1992 by the Orphan Train Heritage Society of America, Inc.

Brace Farm School, Valhalla, New York

EMIGRATION DEPARTMENT
OF THE

Children's Aid Society of New York.

CENTRAL OFFICE UNITED CHARITIES BUILDING

105 East 22d Street, New York City.

The Society reserves the right to remove a child at any time for just cause.

Date of placing

Name of child Emma Elkins

Age 2 yrs, Jan 2 1901

B. W. TICE, AGENT.

Terms on Which Children are Placed in Homes.

Applicants must be endorsed by the Local Committee.

The child selected may then be taken to the home for mutual acquaintance, but no permanent arrangement will be considered until the home has been visited by the Placing-out Agent of the Society and the necessary papers signed.

Children under 14 years of age if not legally adopted, must be retained as members of the family, schooled according to the Educational Laws of the State and comfortably clothed until they are 18 years old. It is then expected that suitable provision will be made for their future.

Children between 14 and 16 years of age must be boarded and clothed until they are 18 when they are at liberty to make their own arrangements.

Children over 16 years of age may be taken on a mutual agreement witnessed by the Agent of the Society or by a member of the local committee.

Parties taking children agree to make reports of them to the Society twice a year, and to urge the children, if old enough, to write also. Removals of children proving unsatisfactory can be arranged through the local committee or an Agent of the Society, the party agreeing to retain the child a reasonable length of time after notifying the Society of the desired change.

The "Emigration and Placing-Out Department" reported in 1903 that 1,500 children had been removed to the country the previous year.

New York Foundling Asylum
The Work of the Sisters of Charity

In the 1850's and 1860's, infants were being deserted in New York City in large numbers.

The Sisters of Charity began the work of the New York Foundling Asylum in 1869 to care for such babies.

Martin Gottlieb wrote "**The Foundling, The Story of the New York Foundling Hospital**", published in 2001.

Mr. Gottlieb writes, "The work began unheralded on Wednesday, October 5, 1869, in the midst of a noisy, bustling city with too much else on its mind—a huge influx of immigration, stark contrasts between expanding wealth and abject poverty, and the dislocations of the recently concluded Civil War. Two young Sisters of Charity were dispatched from Saint Peter's Church on Barclay Street on a trip uptown to Greenwich Village. They stopped at Saint Vincent's Hospital, where they begged a barrel of coal and a barrel of wood. They traveled a few blocks to a four-story red brick brownstone at 17 East Twelfth Street. They turned the key, surveyed the empty confines, and set out to make them 'convent clean.' The Sisters, Teresa Vincent McCrystal and Ann Alousia Tierney, were met at the door by a supporter, Mrs. Daniel Devlin, and the scrubbing began."

The orphanage filled quickly and a decision had to be made as to what to do with the children.

"Baby Trains" carried infants and toddlers from the doors of the Foundling to new homes across America. This was a way to empty beds and make room for others needing them.

A different placement method was used by the Foundling. They contacted priests who in turn asked their congregations to consider taking one or more orphans. The New York Foundling Asylum (later changed to Hospital) used an indenture form which gave them the right to come into the home and remove the child without going to court if need be.

The Foundling required all families taking a child to raise that child in the Catholic faith.

The families could request a particular "type" of child; hair color, color of the eyes and complexion all figured in to the request. Naturally, they could specify boy or girl and age.

Martin Gottlieb stated that often a row of forty or fifty children only five or six years old, followed by a Sister of

Charity and their helpers carrying infants, would walk through Grand Central Station to board a train. "Each child was immaculately dressed. Each had a ribbon with a number and his or her name sewn to an outer garment. Each had a surname stitched to the inside collar of a coat. Each was headed to a foster family somewhere far away."

History of the New York Foundling Hospital
By Alfred J. Vignec, MD, July 1961

The New York Foundling Hospital, now located in a new, modern building has been in continuous operation for over 90 years. The New York Foundling Asylum, as it was originally known, opened its doors on October 11, 1869; it was the first institution in the United States devoted exclusively to the care of abandoned, neglected or dependent infants, regardless of race or creed. It preceded, by only two years, Chicago's Foundling Home, which was organized by Dr. George Elias Shipman, a well-known New York physician who had migrated to Chicago.

The New York Foundling Asylum was founded by the Roman Catholic Order of the Sisters of Charity of St. Vincent de Paul. It had, as its primary objective, the reduction of the appalling rate of infanticide in New York City, most of the deaths being attributable to exposure. In the first year of operation, 61% of the infants admitted were in extremis. While it may be an exaggeration to say that the streets of New York were covered with dead and dying infants, it certainly would not be an exaggeration to say that it was commonplace. Indeed as late as 1892, according to Thomas Knox, 200 foundlings and 100 dead infants were found on New York City streets.

The first residence of the New York Foundling Asylum was a modest, 4-story brownstone building at 17 East 12th Street. This building was situated on the north side of the street between Fifth Avenue and University Place—a site now occupied by the Aristocrat Garage. The adjoining building, No. 15, is still standing and in use.

It was not long before the quarters at 12th Street proved totally inadequate, and in 1870 the Foundling Asylum was moved to a more commodious building at 3 Washington Square North. This building, looking over Washington Square Park, is at present a well-preserved private residence. In less than a year the new quarters proved inadequate, and in 1872 plans were drawn for the construction of a group of buildings on the block bounded on the north and south by 68th and 69th Streets and on the east and west by Third and Lexington Avenues. This move "so distant from the center of the City" was looked upon by many with great misgivings, but the Foundling was to be housed here for the next 85 years. Geography was not the only problem faced by the venturesome sisters at that time, however, for the Panic of 1873 was in the making and money was extremely difficult to raise; the treasurer's report on January 1, 1872, revealed a balance of 52 cents. Financial stringency was to prove to be a chronic condition, and the work was supported over the years by a sort of economic legerdemain that was a masterpiece of deficit financing. Nonetheless by 1873 the main center buildings and the two connecting wings were ready for occupancy. These were followed in 1880 by St. Ann's Maternity Hospital and in 1882 by the Children's Hospital. These same buildings with interior alterations to meet the changing times, and three additional structures, the Chapel, St. Irene's and the Hillyer Auditorium remained in use until 1958. The increase in physical facilities was more than welcomed, although the Foundling Hospital was destined never to find itself with adequate room to meet the need.

In 90 years of its existence, the Foundling has sheltered 107,286 infants. For many years the most important problem faced by the sisters and attending physicians was one of infant survival, for exposure to the elements was only one of the many hazards that faced the homeless infants. Acute intestinal disorders as well as the contagious diseases reaped a heavy toll. Among the latter, diphtheria, pertussis and syphilis played a leading role, and despite the efforts of the "vaccination physician" supplied by the Board of Health, smallpox was not unknown. Acute ocular conditions added greatly to the morbidity and were a source of much concern. Medical problems were by no means alleviated by the overcrowding because of the heavy demands made on the institution. This was relieved in some measure by placing infants at nurse outside of the institution—the beginning of foster-home placements. The nursing homes supplied the advantages of personal care and a home environment. These, as now, foster homes absorbed the great majority of the infants. At the present time, some 2,000 infants and children are in foster homes supervised by the New York Foundling.

Social work was unheard of in those early years, and the supervision of the infants at nurse was undertaken by the men of the Society of St. Vincent de Paul, a lay Catholic organization dedicated to the care of the sick poor. In addition to these charitable gentleman, a detective, kindly lent us by the Board of Police, rounded out the Social Services Department. At the present time 117 social workers are engaged in the supervision and placement of infants and children in foster homes. A further problem also beset the sisters in their work, that of the homeless mothers who appeared at the doors of the institution with their infants. This facet of the work continued, and the Shelter now has facilities for 36 mothers, annually providing services for about 355.

In the early years, instead of being adopted, children were indentured. The sisters and the foundlings, heeding the advice of Horace Greeley, "went west." In bands of 50, accompanied by two sisters, the children found homes in California, the Dakotas, Minnesota, Wisconsin and the Midwest. This was a daring enterprise; there were only 37 states in the Union; the Indians were still a threat; indeed, Custer's last stand at the Battle of the Little Big Horn was fought in 1876, and the Union Pacific had been only a few years in operation (1869) with single track most of the way beyond St. Louis. Contact and supervision of these children was maintained by the sisters on subsequent trips, by local priests and by prominent citizens.

Adoption succeeded indenture, and the Foundling Adoption Service, one of the largest in the country, if not the largest, now consummated approximately 300 adoptions yearly. From this brief account it is apparent that the work that started with the avowed intention of providing shelter for unwanted infants expanded in many directions, providing medical and well-baby care, adoption and foster-home services and a shelter for mothers. All of these services have as their unifying goal the care of the abandoned, dependent and neglected infant.

Despite the development of these ancillary services which were to make the foundling a multi-functioning organization, mortality in the early years remained distressingly high. Sixty-five and sometimes 70% of the infants admitted yearly were in poor or dying condition. The mortality in the institution during 1874-1876 was 45%. This unjustly resulted in a long-held condemnation of institutions for children. A fact seldom stressed and indeed ignored, was that the mortality of infants placed at nurse outside the institution was 55%. This disparity in mortality was to continue for some time, and the chairman of the Medical Staff, J. B. Reynolds, M.D., seriously questioned the advisability of sending the infants out to nurse. Crowding in the institution, however, was so great that this means of caring for the overflow continued.

The development of hospital facilities, beginning with St. Ann's Maternity Hospital in 1880, attracted some of the foremost physicians of the day. An interesting fact brought to light in a perusal of old medical reports was the cost of obstetric care in the final quarter of the last century. For private cases a "reception fee" of $50 was charged. This covered the doctors' and nurses' fees—The Corporate Practice of Medicine. The weekly rate for private rooms was $6 to $15. The "reception fee" for service cases was $25 and the weekly rate was $3. Because of the increasing demand for services to dependent infants, the maternity hospital was discontinued in 1945.

Many outstanding pediatricians gave of their time and attention to the Children's Hospital facility of the institution.
J. Lewis Smith (served 1874-1897) with Jacobi, was the first to practice pediatrics as a specialty; he served on the staff throughout his lifetime. He was Chairman of the founders committee of the American Pediatric Society and was the second president of the Society.
J. O'Dwyer (served 1874-1898) introduced and perfected the technique of intubation for diptheric laryngitis, by means of which hundreds of lives were saved.
J. Henry Fruitnight (served 1879-1881) was one of the founders of the American Pediatric Society.

34

W. P. Northrup (served 1881-1893) was Professor of Pediatrics at Bellevue.

Ronald J. Freeman (served 1893-1899) succeeded Northrop at Bellevue.

L. Emmett Holt, Sr. (Professor of Diseases of Children at Columbia's School of Physicians and Surgeons) served as an attending physician and subsequently as a consultant. For many years he gave bi-weekly clinics for medical students from Columbia.

John Howland (served on the staff in various capacities from 1899 to 1910) left to become a Professor of Pediatrics at Washington University in St. Louis. Shortly thereafter, he became a Professor of Pediatrics at Johns Hopkins. He was successively a resident, the bacteriologist and finally a pathologist of the institution.

Philip Van Ingen, who was subsequently to become a Professor of Pediatrics at Physicians and Surgeons, served a residency at the Foundling, as did Mathias Nicholl, Professor of Infectious Diseases at Bellevue and Edward R. Park, who was to become Professor of Pediatrics at Johns Hopkins.

In the initial decades of the Foundling, emphasis was on treatment and literally lifesaving nursing care. Currently, the emphasis is on preventive medicine, refinements in infant nutrition and more concern for the effects of emotional deprivation of our charges—hence, our interest in better immunization techniques, superior milk preparations and the establishment of developmental and child-guidance clinics.

This is not to say that we are neglecting methods of treatment and the quality of nursing but rather that we have expanded the scope of our interests and aims.

Written by Dr. Alfred J. Vignec and reprinted by permission in its entirety from *Pediatrics*, Vol. 28, No. 1, July 1961, pages 139-145.

RESEARCH TIP #6:

Building the INVISIBLE ORPHANAGE BY Matthew A. Crenson, ISBN # 0-674-46591-1, published by Harvard University Press in 1998, examines the connection between the decline of the orphanage and the beginnings of welfare. The welfare system replaced the oversight of the asylum, the poorhouses, and the penitentiary with "community" care and supervision.

New York Juvenile Asylum

In the winter of 1842-43, the New York Association for the Improvement of the Condition of the Poor was formed. This Association became the key information retainer for all other charities in the City. By 1850, the Association agreed there was a need for a Juvenile Department to improve the condition of the depraved, neglected and morally exposed children and youth of the City.

Mr. John D. Ross, Corresponding Secretary of the Prison Association and Mr. Solomon Jenner of the Society of Friends, made known that they would ask the State Legislature for a charter for an institution to take care of neglected children. They asked to be chartered with the power to remove children from the guardianship of their parents whenever it could be proved that such parents neglected or were incompetent to take care of them, and to preserve them, during their minority, under the sole care of said corporation.

The Poor Association had taken steps in the same direction so in 1850 the two groups united and presented a bill to the Legislature. It was delayed, sent to the Governor but returned. It seemed they had no place to commit the children to. So the bill was amended and named the Juvenile Asylum, the recipient of any children who might be committed under the said bill. The bill with the amendment, and some slight modifications, was passed on June 30, 1851 and became a law.

Janet Coble wrote an account of the New York Juvenile Asylum and its work in placing-out children, **Children of the Orphan Trains from New York to Illinois and Beyond** in 1994, published by the Illinois State Genealogical Society.

The New York Juvenile Asylum sent children out under an Indenture plan. These children were normally of workable age, six years to eighteen years. The Indenture gave a child the right to a new suit of clothes, a specified amount of money and a new Bible when they became of age.

Janet Coble indexed the annual reports of the New York Juvenile Asylum; printed by the Illinois State Genealogical Society in 1994.

Coble's book includes a history of the New York Juvenile Asylum. The following is taken from Janet Coble's work:

In the winter of 1842-3 the "New York Association for the Improvement of the Condition of the Poor: was formed. Through the organization and efforts of the Association, they became possessed of the most reliable information as to the practical workings of all other charities and benevolent institutions whether in private hands or under the direct patronage and management, in whole or part of municipal government. By degrees, this Association became an important auxiliary of nearly every other well directed effort to benefit the masses and also, a great help to the authorities, not only in the administration of justice, but in promoting the usefulness of the varied agencies under the direction and control of the commissioners of Emigration and the ten Governors.

There was still a group of neglected and degraded children who had not been adequately provided for. By 1850 the Association agreed that there was a need for a Juvenile Department to improve the condition of the depraved, neglected and morally exposed children and youth in the City. This required the erection of a suitable House of Detention. In order to improve the children's condition its object was to remove them from dangerous and corrupting associations and place them in such circumstances as would be favorable to their reform, and tend to make them industrious, virtuous and useful members of society.

By January 1853, the New York Juvenile Asylum opened a House of Reception at 109 Bank Street. Soon afterwards a building at the foot of 55th Street was rented. By 1856, 35 acres of ground on 175th Street, near the High Bridge was purchased and a new building was erected to house at least 500.

In 1859 the House of Reception was moved to No. 71 East Thirteenth Street. Children sent by the Magistrates came there and were held ten days until it could be ascertained whether their parents, guardians or protectors would take them away and make suitable provisions for them, or if not, they would be kept, made clean and familiarized with the new state of things in which they found themselves placed, preparatory to being sent to the Asylum. There it was expected that they would remain until discharged to their friends or sent to a home in the country. Only children between the ages of 7 and 14 years were accepted.

Chicago was chosen as a site for the Placing Agency in 1850 where it remained until 1972 when the great fire in Chicago broke out. It was then moved to Bloomington, Illinois.

An indenture system was used. In 1861, the State of Illinois legalized the indenture of the New York Juvenile Asylum issued in Illinois. This allowed the Asylum to have legal standing in case any of the stipulations of the indenture were not followed. This protected both the guardian and the child.

In the fall of 1898, the Asylum began sending children to Iowa and other states in the West.

In 1903 the Asylum needed more room for expansion, so the holdings in New York City were sold, and land was purchased near Dobbs Ferry, North of the City. There a larger facility was built and still functions as the Children's Village. This same year (1903) the Western Placing Agency closed. Arrangements were made with the Illinois Children's Home and Aid Society to handle placing out and visitation. In 1907 and 1908 no children were sent west. From this point on, any children would be sent out by the Children's Aid Society.

RESEARCH TIP #7:

To order a copy of the Coble index, contact the Illinois State Genealogical Society at:

ISGS Illinois State Archives Building
P. O. Box 10195
Springfield, IL 62791-0195

Or contact your local library.

American Female Guardian Society
Home For the Friendless

The American Female Guardian Society had its origin in this city, [New York City] in the spring of 1834. It was at a period of then unprecedented interest in Christian work. The Church at large had been greatly revived, and aroused to the responsibility of individual effort to save the perishing. Tract societies, temperance societies, local benevolent societies for specific objects in churches, and associated efforts in behalf of missions to the heathen, had become widely extended, and at length the eyes of the Christian community had rested upon the fact that, in our great metropolis, there was a hidden moral leprosy, an unseen desolation, affecting the well-being of thousands, blighting character and hope, and blotting out all that was once lovely and of good report.

The picture of this fearful moral ruin was made so vivid by facts and figures and personal observation, as deeply to impress the minds of the early workers in this association. The question, "What can be done to save some of the vast hecatomb of victims, and prevent the young and unguarded from treading in the same dark path," so followed them by day, and disturbed their rest by night, that they could only find relief in prayer and work. They were mothers, and these were somebody's children.

In 1877, Mrs. S. R. I. Bennett wrote a book titled "**Woman's Work Among the Lowly.**" It was a **Memorial Volume of the First Forty Years of the American Female Guardian Society and Home For The Friendless**. At that time, the Society was located at 29 East 29th St. in New York City. *Origin of the Society*(above in bold print) is taken directly, word for word from Mrs. Bennett's book.

The aim of the AFGS was to "remedy" or "prevent" the evils that befell females of their era.

During the first decade, beginning in 1834, the Society assumed the responsibility of publishing a periodical known as the **Advocate and Family Guardian**. Its first design was to exalt the law of God, and thus prevent its violation--to guard the domestic hearth from the invasion of the Spoiler, thus preventing the fall of the innocent; and as far as practicable, to produce such a reform in public sentiment, that the morally-debased should be estimated according to their true character, and made to feel that access to the favor of the virtuous could only be secured by being pure in heart.

The Society opened a house of reception to offer ladies in danger of becoming morally debase to stay but quickly learned this work was better overseen by the Ladies' Benevolent Society and turned it over to them. The ladies of the AFGS turned their attention to the children but continued to publish and sell by subscriptions their publications.

In the Annual Statement of their third year, the AFGS reported being connected to 226 Auxiliaries, and of this number 108 had been formed within the last year. "About 15,000 ladies were connected with these Societies, all pledged to the great principles advocated. The importance of associations like these, bound to this Society and to each other, by the strongest of all ties, the love of Christ, cannot easily be estimated. They afforded pecuniary aid, which was greatly needed to carry forward the plans of the Society, and which could not be relied on, if left to individual, unorganized effort. The moral influence, too, which they asserted, was highly salutary and indispensable to the success of the enterprise.

Within a year, lifetime memberships were established which provided funds to hire two female Missionaries. Mrs. Bennett stated these ladies were granted access in homes where a male Missionary would not be invited in.

At the fourth anniversary, the Society stated the number of Auxiliaries had increased to 361, extending from Maine to Georgia. The **Advocate and Guardian** was being issued semi-monthly and averaged a circulation of 19,000 copies. Some 5,000 copies of **An Appeal to Wives, Mothers, and Daughters** had been distributed.

A major accomplishment during the Society's early years was petitioning city officials to place matrons in the City Prison and at Blackwell's Island. They quickly did as petitioned and two women well suited to the task were appointed to take charge of the female prisoners, in the former place, and other improvements were made in its management. At Blackwell's Island the visitors availed themselves of the advantages thus afforded and expended much time and effort in labors for the prisoners. A weekly prayer meeting was sustained.

In the Annual statement at the close of the first decade we find: *"During the year sixty-three children, chiefly between the ages of one and eight years, were given to the Society, and fifty-four have been provided with homes in Christian families. With few exceptions they have been adopted by those who have taken them."*

By now the ladies felt they needed a physical structure to operate from and to provide shelter for children in need of homes. They located a house at Second Street and First Avenue.

Every dollar secured in a fund-drive to build a building was reserved so the furnishings for the house had to be donations and so the house and supplies to operate it came from Society members and their friends.

A matron and helpers were secured and little groups of Home children brought in from scattered families, where they had been gathered for shelter and temporary care. Monthly, weekly and sub-committee meetings were now appointed.

This hired house was occupied from July 1847 until December 1848. Gathering donated funds, the ladies acquired a site on East 30th Street and on May 5, 1848, the cornerstone was laid, with appropriate ceremonies, in the center of an almost vacant block, well shaded with trees and shrubbery. It would become a shelter for the friendless, and here the destitute and the worthy were to find a home.

The New York State Legislature passed an Act to Incorporate the American Female Guardian Society April 6, 1849 and in February, 1854, the Society opened its first Industrial School, located in the Townsend building, West 35th St and Broadway. Over the door of the House of Industry and Home for the Friendless was placed a sign that read:

Home Industrial School..............Open from 9 A.M. to 3 P.M.
Come learn to sing, come learn to read,
Come learn to work for what you need

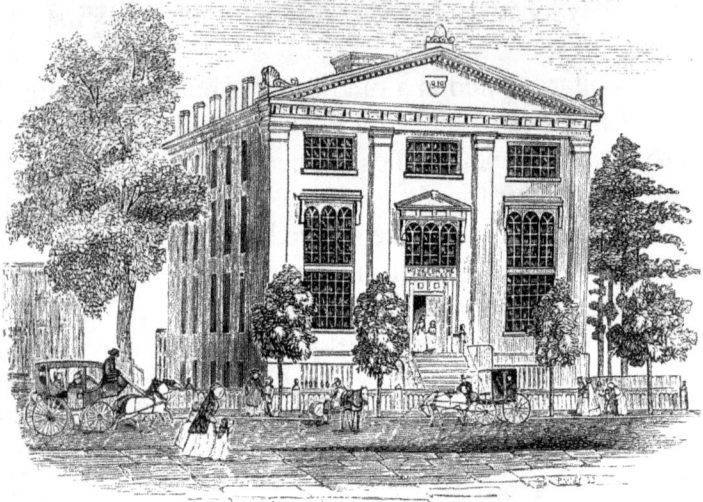

HOME FOR THE FRIENDLESS.

Extracts From the First Report of
First Home Industrial School

From the opening of the School, February, 1854, to the present time, about four hundred vagrant girls have come within the circle of its influence. A number have been removed to permanent homes, in either city or country; and several to the care and shelter of the "Home for the Friendless."

An efficient teacher is employed, and in addition to her labors, about sixty ladies voluntarily render their services; each lady having her own class and hour, one or more days in the week. The morning is devoted to moral and mental instruction; a plain lunch is provided for the scholars, and the afternoon is employed in sewing. The improvement which has been made during the year by many of the children, has been very satisfactory, and in many instances, remarkable. About forty scholars are now able to read intelligibly, many of whom did not know even the alphabet a few months since.

During the year upward of six hundred garments have been made by the children, and about one thousand have been distributed among them and the poor families to which they belong. A system of merit-marks has been adopted, and doubtless does much to secure the interest and prompt attendance of the children. They seem ambitious to earn their own clothing by the two-pence per day marks of approval. At the end of each week these marks are reckoned up, and tickets of the nominal value of from one to ten cents each, are distributed among the deserving children, to be redeemed in clothing.

One hundred and fifty-five Home children and adults were placed in New York, New Jersey, Ohio, Wisconsin and Illinois.

In 1860, on April 14th, the Society was notified that the State of New York approved $10,000 to be used in the work of the organization.

By the close of 1861, four Industrial Schools were being operated under the leadership of the AFGS.

In the report of 1875 and 1876, the Employment Aid Department stated home workers had been supplied with sewing machines and the Society paid these ladies weekly for their garments. One gentleman loaned 44 sewing machines to the Society for these ladies to use. During this two-year period, 100 poor ladies had sewn 1,780 garments for which they were paid $400.99. The AFGS spent $262.99 for material and had sold $70.00 worth of articles.

RESEARCH TIP# 8:

In 1994, records of the Home For the Friendless were saved by Tom Riley of New City, New York and offered by the Rockland County Historical Society on loan to the Orphan Train Heritage Society of America, Inc. to index by Mary Ellen Johnson and to archive.

This ongoing task has resulted in an index of over 50,000 children and is growing daily. The index and copies of actual records are now being made available to persons seeking family information.

Chicago Orphan Asylum

Chicago was a town of 350 persons in 1833 when incorporated and in a scant sixteen years (1849) it grew to just under 30,000. Due to the accessibility to Lake Michigan, the Erie Canal and the Illinois and Michigan canals it became a commercial center.

The first Almshouse, built before 1835, housed the sick, insane and paupers.

The cholera epidemic of 1849 became so bad, President Tyler proclaimed August 3rd as a day of national "Fasting, Humiliation and Prayer." The previous day, a Chicago newspaper published a list of thirty dead, the highest number of cholera victims in one day to date. Many children were orphaned when one or both parents died during the epidemic.

Rev. Elisha Tucker (pastor of the First Baptist Church) presented a plan; *It is the duty of the citizens of Chicago to establish without delay an asylum for the support and benefit of the orphan and destitute children of our City.* Two committees were appointed and on August 7, 1849, eight orphans were given to the care of Mrs. Hanson who had temporarily been engaged as a matron at 73 Michigan Avenue. November 5, 1849, the People of the State of Illinois, represented in the General Assembly, passed Section 1—and the Chicago Orphan Asylum became an official institution.

Important reference tools in researching the Chicago Orphan Asylum are the **Annals of the Chicago Orphan Asylum; from 1849-92** written by Mrs. Charles Gilbert Wheeler and published by the Board of Trustees in 1892. and **Children of Circumstance; A history of the first 125 years (1849-1974) of Chicago Child Care Society** written in 1976 by Clare L. McCausland, printed by R. R. Donnelly and Sons Company of Chicago, Illinois.

Researching children placed-out by the Chicago Orphan Asylum is difficult because only 300 documents relating to the period 1872-1900 are available. Of this number 25 boys and 2 girls were indentured and 273 were adopted. The Adoption Act of 1867 facilitated adoptions. In 1884 the Chicago Orphan Asylum stopped using the indenture form and used the new "Articles of Agreement" when placing children.

To locate information about children living in the Chicago Orphan Asylum (Chicago Child Care Society) it is necessary to know the various locations of the institution before attempting to view census records. Some of these locations were:

- 308 N. Michigan Ave. (west side of the Avenue between Lake and Water Streets)
- Wells St. (between Van Buren and Harrison)
- Adams St. (between State and Dearborn)
- 2228 South Michigan Ave.

RESEARCH TIP # 9:

Newberry Library in Chicago and the Allen County Library in Indiana hold excellent genealogical records.

One way of locating information about a particular Orphan Train Rider is to find obituaries of the Rider or family members where names of survivors are often listed and the towns they lived in at the time. Also, contacting the funeral home who took care of the deceased will often lead to learning who paid for the funeral or memorial service. A Yellow Book Directory of Funeral Homes in the United States is available at most libraries in the genealogical department.

New England Home for Little Wanderers
The Boston Connection

To understand the role Boston's social services played in the Orphan Trains movement, it is necessary to read Peter C. Holloran's book, **Boston's Wayward Children; Social Services for Homeless Children 1830-1930**.

Holloran's work is thorough and written in layman's terms for easy understanding.

On page 122, Holloran writes that the NEHFLW was established to care for the children of Civil War veterans by the Boston Methodists in 1865. By 1867, nine orphans had been sent to the Midwest on orphan trains.

The **Kokomo Gazette Tribune**, Kokomo, Indiana, October 14, 1889 printed the following article on page 2.

HOMES FOR THE HOMELESS
New England's Little Wanderers Warmly Welcomed
Sixteen Bright Children Given a Chance in Life

Rev. V. A. Cooper, Supt. of the Home for Little Wanderers, Boston, Mass., Mrs. C. H. Minor, Matron for the same, Miss Alice Cushing of the nursery department, and Rev. S. S. Cummings, missionary agent, arrived in this city Saturday bringing along with them twenty-four of the Home's children. These little ones range in age from the babes less than two years old to bright boys and girls as old as eleven years. The entire party was guests of the Clinton House during their stay and a more beautiful, better mannered lot of children would be difficult indeed to find anywhere. Their model deportment bespoke the excellent training they had enjoyed at the Home.

This institution is one of the noblest of New England's benefactions. It was founded in Boston, May 1865, by ten benefactors who contributed $5,000 each to its endowment. Since that time its support has been from public charity, and Supt. Cooper says it has never failed for want of funds to meet all its wants. He declares with pious eloquence that it is the Lord's home and is sustained by His unfailing providence. The plan of the Home's work is to accept homeless children and train them to fit into refined homes which are provided them after the manner exercised in this city.

Revs. Cooper and Cummings preached Sunday from the Methodist Congregational, Friend's and Christian pulpits in this city and their children supplied the music in their sweetly charming way, winning many friends by their beautiful childlike manner. All these services were largely attended and it was apparent that the little home-seekers would have no difficulty in winning places in the hearts and homes of

46

our people. Their child-like innocence, their cultivated manners, their tender young lives had already won them the warm affection of many hearts and insured them a cordial reception and affectionate welcome in many homes.

A large audience assembled at the M. E. church at 9:00 o'clock this morning. Some were there to seek the little homeless, others to look well to it that they were well provided for, all with hearts full of sympathy and a manifest tenderness of sentiment, which is the highest possible tribute to our humanity. When the twenty-four little ones filed into the church they were safely lodged in a multitude of people most friendly inclined toward them.

After a brief religious service the work of assigning them began. It was an affecting scene as the little children parted companionship and tore asunder the ties that had linked them in child-like affection, the purest, the truest the most lasting on earth.

Their eyes silvered with tears as they separated to enter the attachments of their new homes and hundreds looked sympathetically on, deeply touched by the affecting scene.

Homes have been obtained for the following:

Mary G. Ring, two years old, with J. C. and Mrs. Blacklidge.

Jennie C. Steele, six years old, with H. H. and Mrs. Stewart.

Arthur Steele, (brother) four years old, with Miles R. and Mrs. McBeth

Charles J. Steele, (another brother) two years old, with John and Mrs. Nesbit.

Marion E. Steele, (sister) ten years old, with J. G. and Mrs. Hockett.

Ida M. Smith, nine years old, with Thos. and Mrs. Huston

Elizabeth B. and Delbert H. Smith, (brother and sister of above) five and seven years old respectively, with Dr. and Mrs. J. McL, Moulder.

Walter Gould, six years old, with A. K. and Mrs. McElwee. Has a brother and sister at Denver, Miami County.

Ira G. Clark, four years old, with Henry and Mrs. Edwards.

George A. Whitman, three years old, with Wm. A. and Mrs. Stanley, Cassville, Ind.

Wm. H. Burding, twelve years old, with W. P. and Mrs. Sellers.

Lena Pope, ten years old, with James and Mrs. Watson.

Nina Fairbanks, five years old, with George and Mrs. McGowan.

Harrold Palph, thirteen years old, with G. E. and Mrs. Mack.

All these children are admirably placed and will gladden the most excellent homes, reciprocating with the unequalled wealth of childhood's charm and affection. There are eight little ones yet waiting for homes and they will be here until provided for.

The representatives of the Home in charge of the children impress observers with their eminent fitness for the discharge of such duties. Revs. Cummings and Cooper, though somewhat advanced in years, are yet young in spirit and rich in sympathy for childhood. Mrs. Minor has been the Home's efficient Matron for many years and it would be next to impossible to find another lady so well adapted to the work, *while Miss Alice Cushing, of the nursery department of the Home, is unequalled.*

October 15, 1889

Little Wanderers

Rev. Mr. Cummings went to Peru last evening and returned today with two nice little boys, Herbert Stygles, aged 13 and Willie Stoddard, aged nine. Circumstances made it necessary that they should be removed from the families in which they were placed last May, and where they were contented and well cared for. Up to this hour there are six children for whom good homes are wanted. Having placed so many of the company here Supt. Cooper is reluctant to take these few to some other town. The children may be seen at the M. E. church until further notice.

October 16, 1889

(No headline)

There is one feature in the distribution of the little waifs in our midst this week that calls for the deepest sympathy. The brightest and handsomest children were in great demand and were given homes in our best families, while a few not so prepossessing or attractive in appearance, nor so bright intellectually, perhaps, as the others, find no one to take them into their homes. Young as they are, these little wanderers recognize this and feel the humiliation, though it is no fault of their own. With eyes dimmed with appealing tears for home and protection they are passed by because of some insignificant physical or mental shortcoming until they feel that nobody cares for them, or entertains the slightest interest in their future welfare. And in their knowledge of the reasons for this lies their pitiable and poignant grief.

.October 17, 1889 the **Kokomo Gazette Tribune** ran a story that stated Walter Gould, six years old, was taken to Denver where he has a sister and brother. It also stated:

Charles A. Patterson, two years old, with George and Mrs. McGowan;

George Shultz, eleven years old, with D. T. and Mrs. Reiff; Christie Shultz (brother of the above) eight years old, with B. F. and Mrs. Redmond.

James McDonald, eleven years old with George W. and Mrs. Landon

Charles Metcher, ten years old, with B. F. and Mrs. Harness

Rachel Morrison, four years old, with Mrs. Mary Clore

Margaret Morrison (sister of above) eight years old, with   Miss Katie Kellar

Henry Keenan, ten years old, with Jesse Ault.

Willard Stoddard, 10 years old, with J. M. and Mrs. Darnall.

Herbert Stygles, 12 years old, was taken to Russiaville to find a home.

Kokomo Gazette Tribune

October 18, 1889, page 2

To Little Wanderers' Friends

Last Saturday evening, the 12th, I arrived in Kokomo with twenty-four homeless children. Two have been added to the company from Peru. Now they are all placed in good families under an agreement that they will be treated as sons and daughters. They are not legally adopted but may be; but are to be treated as though born in these families. We have become deeply interested in these children. Thursday the matron and myself visited as many of the homes as possible. We were greatly pleased.

We have not sought for homes of wealth, although providentially some have found such, but I have reason to believe that as good character, governmental power and parental love may be found in the humblest as in the wealthiest homes, and it is the elements of family life which develop character, and it is character we want our children to have—moral and Christian character. I thought as we passed from house to house and saw how happy the friends are who have taken children to be as their own, can I do anything more to insure their continued happiness. So by the kindness of the editor I give you my advice.

Teach your little boy or girl to obey you in every little thing. Do not say you cannot make them mind, you can if you will. They have been taught obedience in the Home, not by cruelty, but by firmness. Now they must be taught to obey you.

Teach them gratitude. Institutional education can teach them this but very imperfectly. Everything is done for them there and they cannot do much in return. Now patiently teach them to do for you. They have not been accustomed to work, you must teach them. It is due you that they appreciate what you do for them, but they must learn it little by little.

Do not allow them to run the streets—to be out evenings and you not know where they are. The education of the streets is all bad for children.

Do not pity and pet them until they begin to get the upper-hand of you, for then a time will come when you will be obliged to turn over a new leaf and try to bring them back into subjection, and you will have a difficult job on hand.

Read over your agreement and keep it. It has been wisely drawn up. Whenever a difficult and doubtful case comes up, as yourself, "what would I do if the were my born child?" That thing do.

Exercise a firm, consistent, Christian family government and do not forget you have God to help you.

I return my sincere thanks to you, to the Christian ministers, to the committee who have most judiciously and faithfully helped me in selecting these good homes and protected me from placing children

*with incompetent and improper persons, and to the Christian ladies
and kind friends who have so generously entertained the children.*

*A more cordial reception has never been accorded us in any place
and I feel especially grateful to the press; it has helped us in many
ways.*

V. A. Cooper

RESEARCH TIP #10:

Newspaper articles of the time are excellent resources for
documenting such events. In one such newspaper article, mention n
was made of a child the agent had taken from residents of a town he
was delivering orphans to and the agent would be placing the child
in another state. This is how we learned that not all Orphan Train
Riders came out of the East. In this instance, the child was taken
from Kansas to Arkansas where a home was found for the child.

Little Wanderers' Advocate

Vol. XLIV.   Boston, Mass., August, 1908   No. 3

LITTLE WANDERERS' HOME
202 West Newton St.

THE LITTLE WANDERERS' ADVO-
CATE is devoted to the interest of, and
published quarterly by, The New England Home for Little Wanderers at
202 West Newton Street, Boston, Mass.,
and sent to subscribers for one dollar per year.

50

Home for Destitute Catholic Children

The Archives of the Archdiocese of Boston has a transcript history of the Home for Destitute Catholic Children and will be happy to answer any questions about the records. The Archives will provide specific information on individuals where names and reasonably accurate dates are known, but it cannot conduct extensive research. The Archives also has the records of the 19th century Catholic orphanages in Boston and more information on these can be found in **Guide to the Archives of the Archdiocese of Boston** by James M. O'Toole.

Records show that in 1883 and early 1884 four groups of children were sent to Reverend George Sheehan in Welshtown, Yankton County, Dakota. They were sent on July 22, 1883; September 4, 1883; December 16, 1883 and May 26, 1884. In many cases the families taking the children are named in newspaper articles. Descendants of people who show up in the 1900 census in the Dakotas, Iowa or Nebraska, born in Massachusetts could possibly have been Orphan Train Riders sent west by the Home for Destitute Catholic Children.

RESEARCH TIP #11:

Peter Holloran's book, <u>Boston's Wayward Children</u> pages 110-115 describes the Home for Destitute Catholic Children. Holloran's book also covers the Jewish children beginning on page 157. By 1900, 7.1 percent of Boston's population was Jewish.

Jewish Orphanages

In 1994, Brandeis University Press (Hanover, NH) published a work by Reena Sigman Friedman titled "<u>These Are Our Children; Jewish Orphanages in the United States, 1880-1925.</u> The following information is taken from this publication.

Only seven institutions for the care of destitute, neglected, and delinquent children existed in the United States before 1800. The first was in New Orleans, Louisiana, in 1729, founded by the sisters of the Ursuline Convent to care for the children orphaned by the Natchez Indian massacre.

Between 1801 and 1851 about seventy-one orphanages were founded in the United States. At this time, the "mixed almshouse" remained the primary means of caring for dependent children and adults. However, in the decade following the Civil War a campaign was launched to remove dependent youngsters from the bleak, unsanitary environments and pernicious influences of the "mixed almshouses."

William Letchworth, a member of the New York State Board of Charities in the 1870s wrote a series of reports detailing the inhumane and degrading conditions that existed in the state's almshouses. This brought about passage of the landmark New York State Children's Law of 1875. This law mandated the removal of all children aged three to sixteen (except for those with physical or mental defects) from the almshouses, and their placement in separate children's institutions. Hopes were this law would provide a system of boarding homes for dependent children in private homes, but instead it served to promote more widespread institutionalism of dependent children.

In the years following the 1893 depression, nearly one in thirty New York City children lived in institutions, most at the public's expense. One key reason for this dramatic increase in institutions was the law stipulated children to be placed in institutions of the same religious faith as their parents.

The Children's Aid Society was one of the most extensive Protestant organizations for the care of children and viewed as being "bitterly sectarian" by Catholic and Jewish citizens.

Concerned about this state of affairs, the New York Catholic Protectory, established in 1862, became the largest children's institution in the United States, if not in the whole world.

Motivated by the same concerns as their Catholic counterparts, groups of Jewish philanthropists in various American cities organized to establish separate asylums for orphaned, deserted, and destitute Jewish children.

The Hebrew Orphan Asylum (HOA), established in 1860, became the largest institution for the care of dependent Jewish children in the United States, and the largest Jewish institution of its kind in the world. They maintained orphanages in Charleston, New Orleans,

Philadelphia, New York City, Cleveland San Francisco, Baltimore, Newark, Brooklyn, Rochester, Atlanta, Boston, Chicago, Milwaukee and Cincinnati.

The Jewish Foster Home of Philadelphia (JFH) began experimenting with an extensive boarding-out program which included widow's pensions. The Orphans' Guardian Society of Philadelphia was founded in 1868 to place Jewish orphans in supervised private homes.

In 1896, the New York State Legislature mandated that every incorporated child care facility hire a physician to examine children regularly and report his finding to the Board of Health, and that local boards of health supervise sanitary conditions and statistics on infectious diseases in the institution. Children suffering from contagious diseases on admission were required to be isolated in an infirmary until they were cured.

A report in 1919 stated one out of every four children admitted to an institution was a deserted child.

From 1860 until 1922, the Hebrew Orphan Asylum had served 13,506 children.

The Cleveland Jewish Orphan Asylum, by 1920, had a "follow-up" program for their discharged children. It was provided by individual board members as well as a paid staff. Alumni Associations meetings were held once a month and all alumni were welcome to attend. Also, the CJOA placed graduates and provided them with financial aid where necessary.

The cottage institution established in 1912 by the Hebrew Sheltering Guardian Society in Pleasantville was widely recognized as a model in the child welfare field.

Throughout Friedman's text, references are made to the follow-up programs of support for their charges. When boys were indentured to learn a trade, an appointed guardian checked on him frequently. If his wages did not meet his needs, they were supplemented by the Jewish community. The same with girls; until their supervisor was satisfied the child had matured enough to stand on "his own two feet" he (or she) would be cared for.

Strong religious training was very important in Jewish orphanages. This may account for the extended follow-up care.

Many orphanage alumni harbored warm feelings for the institution in which they were raised. Several regarded their fellow inmates as their true siblings. Childhood memories and common experiences forged bonds that were not easily broken.

One alumnus observed that, to a large degree, relationships with other youngsters compensated for the infrequent contact with parents and relatives. They made friends; a big family situation. He summed it up by saying, "Our alumni association is a network of siblings who meet regularly, hold reunions, and help one another in all the ways that a biological family would."

They stayed in touch over the years and became family to each other.

RESEARCH TIP #12:

The book, <u>These Are Our Children; Jewish Orphanages in the United States, 1880-1925</u> is available on interlibrary loan. For a number of years it was believed that no Jewish children were sent west on orphan trains but several found their biological parents to have surnames such as Cohen, Goldberg, Stein, etc. Contact the Jewish Genealogical Society for more information at:

JGS, Inc.
15 West 16th St.
New York, NY 10011
Tel. (212)294-8326
Email   <u>info@jgsny.org</u>

Five Jewish Synagogues are named in the New York Illustrated New Revised Edition, 1876. They were:

Emanuel Temple, corner of 43rd St. and Fifth Avenue
Abawath Chesed, corner of Lexington Avenue and 55th St.
Anshar Chesed, corner of Lexington and 63rd Avenue
Beth El, 248 W. 83rd
Andereth El, 248 West 33rd

Travelers Aid Society

Founded in the 1880's, The Travelers Aid Society is a social service for persons who are in difficulty when traveling or who are newcomers to a community. They provide counseling and helps people obtain clothing, food, jobs, job training, medical aid, shelter and other assistance.

The Travelers Aid Society provides service to more than a million persons each year in the United States. These include the elderly, runaways, immigrants, children traveling alone and the unemployed.

Internationally there are over 800 societies in Canada, Mexico, Puerto Rico, and the United States serving approximately 3,000 communities.

The Los Angeles agency of the Travelers Aid Society was formed in 1922, incorporated in 1944.

Recently the Travelers Aid in Los Angeles sent photos of children who passed through their doors in the 1920's. It is believed that these children were Orphan Train Riders who were being relocated and spent a short time under the care of the Traveler's Aid.

Salvation Army

Little is known about placement of children through the connections of the Salvation Army. One lady has come forward to tell her story and she was placed by the Salvation Army in Colorado.

As time goes on, information on more institutions and more placing agencies will be located. This is why it is so important to maintain a central clearinghouse of information so the material can be assembled and given to others as they need to know it.

RESEARCH TIP #13:
The Internet will probably be the best source for more information on The Traveler's Aid Society and the Salvation Army.

Names Change Records in New York

Many immigrants to New York legally changed their names in order to simplify the spelling, or to adopt an "American" sounding name. Prior to 1875 a change in a personal name could be accomplished through a special act of the Legislature. In Addition, an 1847 statute authorized a court proceeding for the same purpose. Any person over age 21 could petition the judge of a county-level court to issue an order changing his or her name. From 1861 through 1912, lists of names changed by the courts (stating the old and new names, date of change, and court ordering the change) were published in the annual session laws of the Legislature. The court order changing a personal name is recorded in the county clerk's office in the county where the person resides. The name changes published in the session laws are indexed in each volume. Name changes by the Legislature and the courts are also listed in **General Index to the Laws of the State of New York, 1777-1901** (Albany, 1902), Vol. 2, pp. 1309-87; and in a supplement, 1902-1907 (Albany, 1908), pp. 469-567. Orders for name changes filed in the New York County court of Common Pleas are abstracted in Kenneth Scott's work **Petitions for Name Changes in New York City, 1848-1899** (correctly 1848-1889) published by the National Genealogical Society, Publication # 53, Washington, 1984, according to Joan Edelstein.

Chapter Four:
RESEARCH AND RESOURCES

Is There An Orphan Train Rider In My Family?
There are three questions to answer in making this determination.

1. Was the person I believe may have been an Orphan Train Rider born and old enough to travel between the years of 1854 and 1929?
2. Was this person found in early records to have been born in New York, Boston, Chicago or Philadelphia?
3. Did this person grow up in another state with a family having a different surname?

If all three answers are "yes" there is a good possibility that he or she was an Orphan Train Rider.

Overall estimates lead us to believe that over 200,000 children were part of this movement in the 75 years it operated. Today, there would be between 35,000,000 and 40,000,000 descendants living in America.

If your Rider was raised in the Catholic faith and was relocated (while still an infant) from an eastern city to the Midwest, he or she probably came from the New York Foundling Hospital.

If the child was Protestant, between the ages of two and 12 years) he or she could have been placed by the Children's Aid Society. They simply stated the child was to be taken to Sunday School without specifying a particular faith. If the child was between 7 and 14 years of age when relocated between 1854 and 1910, the New York Juvenile Asylum may have been involved in the placement.

Other organizations, institutions and charities placed children using the same methods but on a much smaller scale. The Minnesota Home Society sent children out to find new homes. The same practice took place in the Dakotas and in other states.

Where Did The Orphans Go?

The first group of children sent out of New York City by the Children's Aid Society went to Dowagiac, Michigan, leaving New York City on September 20, 1854. This group of 46 children traveled by boat and by railroad to reach their destinations.

The First Orphan Train Riders
(Reprinted from original text)

On Wednesday evening [September 1854], with emigrant tickets to Detroit, we started on the Isaac Newton for Albany.....forty-six boys and girls from New York, bound westward, and to them homeward. They were between the ages of seven and fifteen, the majority of them orphans—as bright, sharp, bold, racy a crowd of little fellows as can be grown nowhere out of the streets of New York. Two of them had slept in nearly all the station-houses in the city. One, a keen-eyed American boy, was born in Chicago—an orphan now, and abandoned in New York by an intemperate brother. Another, a little German Jew, had been entirely friendless for four years and had finally found his way into the Newsboys' Lodging House. Dick and Jack's mother died three weeks ago in Bellevue Hospital; their father is intemperate, and an older brother has recently been sentenced to Sing Sing. Another boy had just landed in New York from Liverpool. He had been working about the docks, sleeping in a wooden box, much too small for him. Now and then the sailors gave him a cast-off garment, which he wrapped and tied about him, till he looked like a walking rag-bundle.

As we steamed off from the wharf the boys gave three cheers for New York and three more for Michigan. All seemed as careless at leaving home forever as if they were on a target excursion to Hoboken. We had a steerage passage, and after the cracker-box and gingerbread had passed around, the boys sat down in the gang-way and began to sing. Their full chorus attracted the attention of the passengers, who gathered about and soon the captain sent for us to come to the upper saloon. There the boys sang and talked, each one telling his own story separately, as he was taken aside, till ten o'clock, when the captain gave them all berths in the cabin. Meanwhile, a lady from Rochester, had selected a little boy for her sister, and a merchant from Illinois, had made arrangements to take the boy from Liverpool for his store.

At Albany, we found the emigrant train did not go out till noon; and the intervening six hours raised a problem. The Albany street boys tried hard to coax some of ours away but our boys turned the tables on them, told them of Michigan and when we were about to

58

start, several came up bringing a stranger with them. There was no mistaking the long, thick, matted hair, unwashed face, the badger coat, and double pants flowing in the wind—a real snoozer. "Here's a boy what wants to go to Michigan, sir; can't you take him with us?" There is no resisting the appeal of the boys, and the importunate face of the hopeful young vagrant won our sympathy at once. If left to float here a few months longer, his end is certain. "Do you think I can go, sir?" "Yes, John, if you will have your face washed and hair combed within half and hour." Under a brisk scrubbing, his face lighted up several shades, but the twisted, tangled hair, matted for years, will not yield to any amount of washing and pulling—barber's shears are the only remedy. So a new volunteer is added to our regiment.

At the depot we worked our way through the babel of at least one thousand Germans, Irish, Italians, Norwegians, etc. The motley mass rushes into the cars, and we are pushed into one already full—some standing, a part sitting in laps, and some on the floor under the benches; crowded to suffocation, a freight car without windows, rough benches for seats, and no back; no ventilation except through the sliding doors, where the little chaps are in constant danger of falling through. Irishmen passed around bad whiskey and sang bawdy songs; Dutchmen and women smoked and sang, and grunted and cursed; babies squalled and nursed. Night came on, and we were told that passengers furnish their own lights. For this we were unprepared, and so we tried to endure darkness, relieved here and there for a few minutes by a lighted pipe.

In the morning, we were in the vicinity of Rochester; and the children looked, many of them for the first time, upon country scenery.

"What's that, Mister?"

"A corn field."

"Oh, yea, them's what makes buckwheaters."

"Look at them cows." (Oxen plowing.)

"My mother used to milk cows."

As we were whirled through orchards loaded with large red apples, their enthusiasm was uncontrolled. It was difficult to keep them within doors. Arms stretched out, hats swinging, eyes swimming, mouths watering, and all screaming, "Oh! Oh! Just look at 'em! Mister, be they any sich in Michigan? Then I'm in for that place; three cheers for Michigan!"

Next we passed a corn field spread over with ripe, yellow pumpkins.

"Oh! Yonder! Look! Just look at 'em!" and in an instant the same exclamation was echoed from forty-seven mouths.

"Jist look at 'em! What a heap of mushmillons!"

"Mister, do they make mushmillons in Michigan?"

"Ah fellers, aint that the country tho'; won't we have nice things to eat?"

"Yes, and won't we sell some, too?"

"Hip! Hip! Boys; three cheers for Michigan!"

We were in Buffalo nine hours, and the boys had the liberty of the town, but were all on board the boat in season. We went down to our place, the steerage cabin, and no one but an emigrant on a lake boat can understand the night we spent...It was the last night in the freight car repeated, with the addition of a touch of seasickness, and of the stamping, neighing, and bleating of a hundred horses and sheep over our heads. But we survived and in the morning we got outside upon the boxes, and enjoyed a beautiful day. The boys were in good spirits, sang songs, told New York yarns and made friends generally among the passengers. Occasionally someone more knowing than wise, would attempt to poke fun at them, whereupon the boys would pitch in and open such a sluice of Bowery slang as made "Mr Would-Be-Funny" beat a retreat in double quick time. No one attempted the game twice.

We reached Dowagiac, in Southern Michigan, three o'clock Sunday morning and the boys spread themselves on the station floor to sleep. At daybreak they began to inquire, "Where be we?" and finding that they were really in Michigan, scattered in all directions, each one for himself, and in five minutes there was not a boy in sight of the depot. By the time I had breakfast nearly ready, they began to straggle back, each boy loaded down---caps, shoes, coat-sleeves, and shirts full of every green thing they could lay their hands upon--- apples, ears of corn, peaches, pieces of pumpkins, etc.

"Look at the Michigan filberts!" cried a little fellow running toward me, holding both hands upon his shirt bosom, which was bursting with acorns. Little Mag brought in a nosegay which she insisted upon sticking in my coat—a mullen-stock and corn leaf, twisted with grass. Several of the boys had had a swim in the creek, though it was a pretty cold morning.

After breakfast, we started for the meeting house, the children with clean happy faces but their clothes badly soiled and torn by the emigrant passage. You can imagine the appearance of our ragged regiment as we filed in. The natives could not be satisfied with staring, and the parson being late, we occupied the time in singing. Their favorite hymn was, "Come, Ye Sinners, Poor and Needy"; and they rolled it out with a relish. It was a touching sight and pocket handkerchiefs were used quite freely among the audience.

At the close of the sermon, the people were informed of The Children's Aid Society. It met with the cordial approbation of all present and several promised to take children. Monday morning the boys held themselves in readiness to receive applications from the farmers. They would watch in all directions, scanning closely every wagon that came in sight, and deciding from the appearance of the driver and the horses, more often from the latter, whether they would go in for that farmer. There seems to be a general dearth of boys, and still greater of girls, in all this section, and before night I had applications for fifteen of my children, applicants bringing recommendations from their pastor and the justice of the peace. Before Saturday they were all gone.

A few of the boys are bound to trades, but most of them insisted upon being farmers, and learning to drive horses. They are to receive a good common school education and one hundred dollars when they are twenty-one years of age. Mag is adopted by a wealthy Christian farmer. Smack the privateer from Albany has a good home in a Quaker settlement; the two brothers, Dick and Jack, were taken by an excellent man and his son, living on adjacent farms. The German boy from the Lodging House will live with a physician.

On the whole, the first experiment of sending children West is a happy one, and I am sure there are places enough with good families in Michigan, Illinois, Iowa and Wisconsin, to give every poor boy and girl in New York a permanent home. The only difficulty is to bring the children to the home.

Note: This account came from The Crusade for Children 1853-1928. In another account of this same trip, it was mentioned that nine of the smallest children were taken to Chicago and sent to Mr. Townsend in Iowa City but the majority were taken in Cass County. This version also stated the church as being Presbyterian, which was also a school house. This account also stated "Landed in Detroit at ten o'clock Saturday night, and took a first-class passenger car on Michigan C. R. R."

A report on the dates and numbers of trips made by agents for the Children's Aid Society are listed in the 1869 annual report:

In 1868, J. P. Brace took:
48 children on February 11;
63 children on March 10;
17 children on April 21;
23 children on May 5;
26 children on July 14;
53 children on August 25;
36 children on October 5;
70 children on November 17;
53 children on December 29; and
26 children on January 12, 1869.
The same year, Mr. E. Trott took:
36 children on March 24;
28 children on May 19;
40 children on August 11;
57 children on September 22;
48 children on November 6;
38 children on December 15 and
36 children on January 26, 1869.

Mr. H. Friedgen took 73 children on February 25 and his 75th trip was April 7, with 40 children.

Mr. C. C. Tracy took 9 children on June 16 and on his 79th trip, October 20, he took 21 children.

C. R. Fry took 14 children on June 2; 32 children on July 28 and 44 children on December 1.

J. Gourley took 32 children on September 8 and 23 children on January 30, 1869.

C. O'Connor took one trip with 45 children on August 4.

J. W. Skinner took one trip with 40 children on June 30, 1868. The statement is made that in 1868 the Children's Aid Society provided homes or employment to 1,273 boys; 692 girls; 155 men and 143 women. Of those numbers Illinois received 533, New York received 468, with 464 remaining in the City. New Jersey took 144 and Iowa took 103. Other states took fewer in numbers.

Orphan Train Riders

At first this method of caring for homeless children was called the "*free-home-placing-out*" program. The fact they rode trains did not have any bearing on the name of the program until Dorothea G. Petrie and James Magnusson authored the book, **Orphan Train**, in 1978, published by The Dial Press in New York City. From this period on, the term "orphan train" has been used liberally.

Mrs. Petrie had taken her mother back home to Dysart, Iowa, the town of her mother's birth, during Dysart's centennial celebration. Her mother had grown up with Ben Pippert who told a most unusual story about his early life. Ben had arrived, with a group of very young children in Dysart on a wintry day in 1894. They had been taken off the train, walked to the town hall and put up for 'adoption' so to speak. People were invited to look the children over and some were taken to live with this new family. Those not chosen were put back on the train to try again at other stops along the route.

Mrs. Petrie writes in the front of her book, "*I was fascinated by his story and in particular by the phenomenon of the 'orphan train.' Two years of research followed, during which the little known, remarkable story of the Children's Aid Society came to light."*

The Petrie and Magnusson book was made into a television movie, **Orphan Train**, and later became available to the public in the form of a VHS videotape.

RESEARCH TIP # 14:
Reader's Digest condensed Books reprinted Petrie and Magnusson's book in the spring 1978 issue. Another "made for television" movie, <u>Home At Last</u> was filmed in 1987 in Nebraska. An Orphan Train Rider, Mary Tenopir, and three of her granddaughters, were "extras" on the set of that movie. Tenopir's story can be found in a book, <u>Tears on Paper</u> written by Patricia Young and Frances Marks in 1990.

Locating Places for the Children

The Orphan Train Heritage Society of America, Inc. maintains a database of information sent by Orphan Train Riders and their descendants. Data is also extracted from newspaper, magazine articles, books and reference materials. It is added to almost daily so the following charts only a small portion of the towns that received children. However, the following destinations have been recognized.

1854- **Connecticutt**: Winchester
    Illinois: Mendota; Metamora; Trivoli
    Louisiana: Mansura; Morgan City
    Michigan: Dowagiac
1855- **Illinois:** DeKalb County; Lincoln; Vermillion County
1856- **Illinois**: Morgan County
    Michigan: Albion
1857- **Iowa:** Sioux City
    Michigan: Albion; Marengo
    New York: Lockport
1858- **Illinois**: Danville
    Michigan: Clinton County
1860- **Illinois**: Champaign County; Fayette County; Sycamore
    Indiana: Colfax; Goshen; Sheffield Township
    Missouri: Green County
    Wisconsin: Oshkosh; Pierce County

1861- **Illinois**: Bond County; Champaign; Fayette County; Mahomet
    Indiana: Connersville; Rushville
    Iowa: Cedar Rapids
    Kansas: Garnett
    Michigan: Lenawee County
    Missouri: Burlington Junction
    Nebraska: Wymore
    Wisconsin: Madison
1862- **Illinois**: Rockford
    Indiana: Middletown
    Iowa: Harrison County
    Louisiana: Baton Rouge
    Ohio: Wyandot County
1863- **Indiana**: Chesterton; Sulphur Springs
1864- **Illinois**: Louisville; St. Clair County; Whiteside County
    Iowa: Andrew
1865- **Connecticut:** Lebanon
    Illinois: Chicago; Gilson; Prairie City
    Iowa: Malcolm
    Kansas: Walton (taken by the mother)
    Maine: Bath
    Massachusetts: Boston; Brighton; Cambridge; Dedham;
      Edgartown; Lawrence; Lowell; Lynn; Milford; Quincy;
      Roxbury; Salem; Sandwich; Shapley; Sterling;
      Tweksbury; Waltham; Woodstock; Worcester
    Michigan: Adrian; Clayton; Detroit; Jonesville; Quincy; Rome;
      Tecumseh
1865- **Minnesota**: Adams
    New Hampshire: Amherst; Salem
    New Jersey: Freehold; Milhaven
    Ohio: Columbus; Putnam; Zaneville
    Vermont: North Windham
1866- **Illinois**: Champaign County; Tolono
1867- **Illinois**: Sunbeam
    Iowa: Estherville
1868- **Illinois**: DeWitt County; Lincoln; Prairie City
    Iowa: Jasper County
    Louisiana: Opelousas or Lake Charles
    Ohio: Drake County
1869- **Illinois**: Mercer County
    Iowa: Fairfield
    Minnesota: LeRoy
    Pennsylvania: Philadelphia
    Wisconsin: Stoughton

The number of miles of railroad tracks in 1850, 9,021, increased to 30,635 by 1860. By 1853, travel by rail was possible from the Atlantic seaboard to Chicago. In 1854, the Chicago and Rock Island railroads connected Chicago to the Mississippi River. May 1, 1869, the golden spike was driven in Promontory, Utah, connecting lines East and West.

From that point on, travel by rail was the least expensive and most efficient (time wise) until the automobile became available to the general public. Up into the 1940's and early 1950's, travelers were still using the railroads as a source of travel.

From the database of the Orphan Train Heritage Society of America, Inc., we find information stating the following towns took Orphan Train Riders for the next decade.

1870- **Arkansas**: Carlisle
    Illinois: Belleville; Paxton
    Kansas: Emporia
    Missouri: Trenton
    Tennessee: Franklin County
    Wisconsin: Janesville

1871- **Illinois:** McDonough County; Mendota; Vermillion County
    Iowa: Hampton
    Missouri: Farmington; St. Louis

1872- **Arkansas**: Little Rock
    Illinois: Industry
    Iowa: Atlantic
    Indiana: Terre Haute
    Kansas: Kearney County

1873- **Illinois:** Hancock County; Macon County; Moultrie County; Shelby County
    Indiana: Marion
    Missouri: Neosho
    Wisconsin: Black River Falls

1874- **Illinois**: Vermillion County

1875- **Colorado**: Colorado Springs
    Illinois: Bement; Lee County; Vermillion County
    Kansas: Tonganoxic
    Louisiana: New Orleans
    Maryland: Ridge
    Michigan: Argentine; Fenton; Holly; Rose Township; Tyrone
    Missouri: Rockport

1876-**Illinois**: Boone County; Chana; DeKalb County; Holcomb;
              Iroquois County; Rochelle
     Iowa: Cherokee; Maquoketa
     Nebraska: Franklin
     New Jersey: Trenton
1877- **Illinois**: Henry County; Louisville
     Iowa: Red Oak
     Missouri: Clinton; Ray County; Roanoke
     Nebraska: Nebraska City
1878- **Illinois**: Alton; Lee County; Whiteside
     Iowa: DeWitt; Floyd County; Vail
     Kansas: Peabody
     Maryland: St. Mary's County
     Missouri: Cooper County; Vandalia
1879- **Illinois**: Kankakee; Will County
     Iowa: Hamburg; Tipton (Cedar County); Wayne County
     Kansas: Parsons; Wamego
     Michigan: Ann Arbor; Jackson
     Virginia: Mineral Water; Prince Edward County

The New York Foundling Hospital sent children to
Maryland, first, then upstate New York before carrying them
to Minnesota, Arizona and Louisiana among other states.

At this point, the "free-home-placing-out" had been going
on for some 25 years and had been brought to the attention
of politicians who debated the good and bad points of the
program.

The question of placing children of Catholic parents into
Protestant homes was bitterly disputed. The Children's Aid
Society did not specify a religion, simply asked the receiving
parents to send the child to Sunday School. The Foundling
Hospital placed their children only in Catholic homes or
homes where the parents agreed to raise the child in the
Catholic faith.

When researching an Orphan Train Rider, never assume
the nationality based on the surname of the child. Many
"foundlings" were truly left lying in one spot or another,
usually where they would be easily found. However, with
only a living baby dressed in some type of clothing and
nothing more to go on, a name was chosen at random for the
child thereby denoting some guess as to the nationality.

Often, even the older children who could walk and talk but found aimlessly wandering the streets would not know their full names. Several were termed "John Doe #1" or "Jane Doe #1" with the pitiful prospects of never having a real name. In the American Female Guardian records, there are even John Doe's and Jane Doe's with numbers up in the twenties meaning several children were found and unnamed.

Where to Look Next

It has now been 150 years since the first group of Orphan Train Riders came "west" out of New York City. It has been 75 since they stopped carrying children to new homes aboard trains. Much documentation has been lost.

In 1995, Carolee R. Inskeep compiled an index of the census records (1870-1925) of the New York Foundling Hospital (ISBN# 0-8063-4590-X) that is a very valuable resource.

If the potential Rider was placed out as an infant or small child between the years of 1875 and 1912, with a Catholic family, it would be wise to search for an Indenture form or Baptismal Certificate. The Baptismal Certificate would be from St. Vincent Ferrer Church in New York City. Babies placed at the Foundling were often baptized there.

If the baby was a "true" foundling, there are no records that will help find biological parentage. However, a medical record of the condition of the child should be found because every baby that came into the care of the Sisters of Charity was examined and certified to not have any communicable disease. The doctors would have not allowed an infected child to be put in a room with others for fear of spreading an illness.

Legal documents were necessary to prove the Foundling had authority to not only care for the child, but to release it for Indenture or adoption.

Searching the Inskeep list we were able to determine that a little girl with the first name of Bianca born in the fall of 1904 was probably Bianca Zigalotti who is listed in the June 1, 1905 census index. The family knew only her first name (given name) and she was raised Catholic. They also knew there were no other women in the adopting family with that first name. Once the name Bianca Zigalotti was a probablilty, the family asked the New York Foundling Hospital to search their records for any information they could possibly have on this little girl who meant so much to them.

For the website of the New York Foundling; simply type in the name and "search."

"**The Foundling**" by Martin Gottlieb, published in 2001, by Norfleet Press Books, New York, New York, is a "must read" for learning about the Foundling and its operations.

The Children's Aid Society is still in existence in New York City and still caring for children. If you believe your Rider came from this Protestant organization, contact Victor Remer, Archivist.

If your Rider arrived in Illinois during the years the New York Juvenile Asylum was placing children, search Janet Coble's book then ask the Orphan Train Heritage Society of America, Inc. (OTHSA) to copy that page from the annual report and send it to you.

An example would be Israel McEwan.

Coble's book lists Israel McEwan as being brought to Kankakee County, Illinois, when he was 14 years old. In 1881 (making his birth ca 1867) where he was placed with Mrs. A. Lanfear in Mantero. This information can be found in the 1882 Annual Report of the NYJA on page 53. Another mention was made of him in the 1884 Annual Report, page 53.

Contact the Illinois State Genealogical Society to purchase a copy of the Coble index or go to your local library. [Address on page 72 of this book.]

Kansas families are in really good hands while researching because Robert Hodge of Emporia, Kansas, indexed a multitude of Kansas newspapers giving accounts of children upon their arrivals in the state. Many list the children by biological name. OTHSA has this index at the Orphan Train Riders Research Center and Museum located in Concordia, Kansas.

Children taken to Louisiana are being recorded by members of L.O.T.S. (Louisiana Orphan Train Society) headquartered in Opelousas, Louisiana.

Iowa Orphan Train Riders' information is being gathered in Delmar, Iowa at the Delmar Depot.

Minnesota Riders information is archived at the Olmsted Historical Society in Rochester, Minnesota.

If you want to know if the state you are searching in has archives in that area, contact OTHSA for an up-to-date list.

Normal genealogical research methods are used to locate biological information. If you are not accustomed to this "new hobby" it would be to your benefit to join a genealogical society and take some beginners classes.

Sometimes children were given their mother's maiden name as a middle name. We found three boys having the same middle name, Watson. Later found this to have been the mother's maiden name.

When researching, don't forget the possible "Canadian Connection." Children crossed borders, with or without families. Sheila Beatty-Krout did extensive research on the Canadian Home Children while researching her father's biological family. To date her work has not been formally published, however, she has shared a great deal of her information with OTHSA's Orphan Train Riders Research Center in Concordia, Kansas.

OTHSA, Inc.
P.O. Box 322
Concordia, KS 66901

Olmsted County Historical Society
1195 West Circle Drive, SW
Rochester, MN 55902
Tel. (507)282-9447
Email – ochs@millcomm.com

Delmar Depot
City Hall
P.O. Box 239
Delmar, IA 52039
Tel. (319)674-4256
Email – fmaharry@mail.delwood.k12.is.us

Orphan Train Heritage Society of America, Inc.

Founded in 1986, incorporated in 1987, The Orphan Train Heritage Society of America, Inc.(OTHSA) moved from the original location in Springdale, Arkansas, to a new permanent home in Concordia, Kansas in July of 2003.

OTHSA maintains a database of Riders at the Orphan Train Riders Research Center and Museum connected to the restored Union Pacific Depot in Concordia. This is the only national center dedicated solely to Orphan Train Riders in the United States.

A newsletter, **CROSSROADS**, is published by OTHSA and is available thorough many libraries and on the web site: http://www.orphantrainriders.com.

OTHSA has also published five books of Orphan Train Riders stories. These are listed in the reference section of this book.

OTHSA, Inc.
P.O. Box 322
Concordia, KS 66901
E-mail: othsa@msn.com
Website:
http://www.orphantrainriders.com
You may contact the author of this book:
Mary Ellen Johnson, Founder of OTHSA, Inc.
4912 Trout Farm Road
Springdale, AR 72762
E-mail: orphantrainlady@cox-internet.com

Chapter Five:
REFERENCES and READING LIST

How The Other Half Lives; Studies Among the Tenements of New York by Jacob A. Riis; originally published in 1890 by Charles Scribner's Sons, New York, reprinted and copyrighted by Dover Publications in 1971. ISBN#0-486-22012-5. Contains 100 photographs and a very educational preface written by Charles A. Madison in 1970. The Appendix gives good statistical reports on the tenement problems and a map of the particular section of New York City where they were located. Contact Dover Publications to order this book or it may be purchased at Barnes & Noble Booksellers.

The Orphan Trains by Annette R. Fry, printed in 1994 by Macmillan Publishing Company as part of their New Discovery Books. ISBN#0-02-735721-X; includes bibliographical references and index. A New York Foundling Hospital Indenture form for a male child is found on page 89. Out of print/available on interlibrary loan.

Children of Orphan Trains from New York to Illinois and beyond compiled by Janet Coble in 1994; published by the Illinois State Genealogical Society is an index of the New York Juvenile Asylum's annual reports . Coble's work includes a chart of the years and numbers of children apprenticed by the NYJA in Illinois totally 5,935.
Mailing address to order a copy:
ISGS Illinois State Archives Building
P.O. Box 10195
Springfield, IL 62791-0195

The Orphan Trains; Placing Out in America by Marilyn Irvin Holt was printed by the University of Nebraska Press in 1992, ISBN#0-8032-2360-9. This book is viewed as being a "must read" for anyone seeking background material for an "orphan train" project. Holt's excellent grasp of the importance of preserving this part of America's history reflects her time and energy spent thoroughly researching her subject. This book is sold by OTHSA in the gift shop in Concordia, Kansas. See address on page 71.

American Reformers 1815-1860 by Ronald G. Walters is part of the American Century Series published by Hill and Wang in New York, a division of Farrar, Strauss and Giroux. Copyrighted in 1978, ISBN#0-8090-0130-6. Walters covers this period of growth (8,400,000 in 1814 to 31,443,321 on the eve of the Civil War) by comparing social, economic and political life in America in a way that is most interesting and informative. Most libraries carry this book or can get it for you.

We Rode the Orphan Trains by Andrea Warren in 2001, published by Houghton Mifflin Company, Boston, ISBN#0-618-11712-1; gives a good accounting of the lives of surviving Orphan Train Riders, or as they are called the "Last Riders." The book abounds with family photographs of Riders along with their personal stories. An excellent book for every home library. Sold by OTHSA and major booksellers.

Children of the Orphan Trains 1854 to 1929 by Holly Littlefield is one in the series of "Picture the American Past" series published by Carolrhoda Books, Inc., Minneapolis; ISBN#1-57505-466-3. This book is written for upper elementary students and adults. It contains a section defining certain words the reader may not be familiar with and an index. Littlefield also lists resources for more reading about the Orphan Trains era. Sold by OTHSA and other booksellers.

Lost in New York by Nathan Silver, published by Random House in 1967; ISBN#0-517-16703-4 is a collection of photographs of buildings and places in New York City. Silver, an Architect, collected photographs of the city's lost buildings that might have never been saved if not for his work. Most libraries carry this book in the reference section.

The Dangerous Classes of New York and Twenty Years' Work Among Them , originally published in 1872, authored by Charles Loring Brace; reprinted by the National Association of Social Workers in 1973, ISBN#0-87101-061-5 is one of the most revealing works about the Children's Aid Society to be found. Brace had the knowledge learned only by being in the center of the work and decision-making process. His burdens and joys are a good study for social workers today. At last contact, NASW was no longer carrying the book for sale.

ORPHAN TRAIN RIDERS; Their Own Stories Series of true stories published by the Orphan Train Heritage Society of America, Inc.; printed by Gateway Press in Baltimore, Maryland.

- Vol. 1 (1992) (Library of Congress Catalog Card # 92-70052) contains 84 stories of the lives of Orphan Train Riders as written by themselves or a family member. The book is 463 pages, fully indexed. First printed in maroon linen hard cover, now reprinted in paperback.
- Vol. 2 (1993) (ISBN 0-9635902-2-7) contains 41 stories of Riders written by themselves or a member of their family. This book also contains a history of how OTHSA began and a story of the life of Charles R. Fry, a western placing agent for the Children's Aid Society
- Vol. 3 (1995) (ISBN 0-9635902-3-5) contains 54 individual stories plus an excerpt from Helen Campbell's 1896 book, "*Darkness and Daylight; Lights and Shadows of New York Life*.

- <u>Vol. 4 (1997)</u> (ISBN 0-9635902-4-3) contains 73 individual stories on 496 pages including index and an epilogue written by Dagmar Zimmer; ***Finding a Place in History: America's Orphan Trains, 1854-1929.***

Journeys of Hope (ISBN# 0-9635-9025-1) is the fifth book in the above series to be published. Printed in 1999 through the financial assistance of Doris Ferguson; the books were donated to OTHSA to sell as a major fundraiser. The book contains 32 stories on 356 pages including an index.

THE NEW YORK FOUNDLING HOSPITAL; An Index to Its Federal, State, and local Census Records by Carolee R. Inskeep published in 1994 by Clearfield Company in Baltimore, Maryland. In addition to the federal census records for 1870, 1880, 1900, 1910 and 1920; Inskeep includes the 1890 New York City Police Census and New York State Census for 1905, 1915, and 1925. Inskeep also indexed the census for the Children's Aid Society but it has not proved to be as helpful as the one for the Foundling.

THE FOUNDLING The Story of the New York Foundling Hospital by Martin Gottlieb, photographs by Claire Yaffa, published in 2001 by Norfleet Press in New York City. This book may be ordered from:
New York Foundling Hospital
590 Avenue of the Americas
New York, New York 10011

THE LOWER EAST SIDE A Guide to Its Jewish Past in 99 New Photographs Text by Ronald Sanders and Photographs by Edmund V. Gillon, Jr. copyrighted in 1979; a photograph on page 80 shows the building housing the Triangle Shirtwaist Factory where the top three floors burned March 11, 1911, killing 146 people. Printed by:
Dover Publications
31 East 2nd St.
Mineola, NY 11501

The Crusade for Children 1853-1928; A Review of Child Life in New York During 75 Years contains a forward by Owen R. Lovejoy, Secretary of the Children's Aid Society. The book is printed by the Children's Aid Society in 1929 and contains many artwork illustrations.

Boston's Wayward Children; Social Services for Homeless Children 1830-1930 by Peter C. Holloran, published by Associated University Presses in 1989, ISBN# 0-8386-3297-1 is an valuable research tool for learning more about the child welfare systems in the United States. Holloran goes into detail about the differences in child welfare programs operated by the Boston Blacks, Jews, Italians, Brahmins and Irish. Extensive chapter note, a bibliography and index make this a very usable tool.

THE GREAT ARIZONA ORPHAN ABDUCTION by Linda Gordon in 1999, ISBN# 0-674-36041-9, closely follows the book, **Foundlings on the Frontier** by A. Blake Brophy published by the University of Arizona Press some years earlier, ISBN# 0-8165-0319-2 Both books detail the account of a forty Irish orphans brought in 1904 to remote Arizona mining camps to be placed with Catholic families by the New York Foundling Hospital. The Caucasian community became alarmed and a fight for the children erupted. A lawsuit eventually settled the matter. The Gordon book is steeped in area research details while the Brophy book centers on the children and the episode.

Orphan Trains THE STORY OF CHARLES LORING BRACE AND THE CHILDREN HE SAVED AND FAILED by Stephen O'Connor in 2001, published by Houghton Mifflin, ISBN# 0-395-84173-9. O'Connor starts his prologue with an account of the first orphan train, the one to Dowagiac, Michigan in 1854. It is a good book to read for information and to study about the life of a man both praised and derided for his work with New York City's homeless children. The book is available through Barnes and Noble Booksellers and other retail outlets.

We Are A Part of History: The Story of the Orphan Trains By Michael Patrick, Evelyn Sheets and Evelyn Trickel, in 1990, ISBN# 0-89865-921-3 by The Lightning Tree Press. The book focuses on Missouri Orphan Train Riders but includes W. P. "Willie" Dunnaway who came to Rogers, Arkansas on an Orphan Train. The book conatins many interviews and family photos. It is an excellent resource and a good addition to a family library. This book may be purchased from OTHSA.

Orphan Trains to Missouri by Michael D. Patrick and Evelyn Goodrich Trickel, 1997, published by the University of Missouri Press, ISBN# 0-8262-1121-6 contains research done at the Western Historical Manuscript Collection in Columbia, Missouri, which houses the Annette Riley Fry collection. This book is sold by OTHSA.

Tears On Paper; Orphan Train History by Patricia Young and Frances Marks, 1990, Library of Congress Catalog Card Number 90-61695 based on interviews with Riders taken to Nebraska. This book is self published and sold by the author and OTHSA.

Woman's Work Among the Lowly by Mrs. S. R. I. Bennett, 1877 published by the American Female Guardian Society. Long out of print, check with antique booksellers to find a copy of this most interesting book. It details early "do-gooders" and their efforts at saving the morals of young ladies from 1837 to 1877, forty years.

ORPHAN TRAIN RIDER One Boy's True Story by Andrea Warren, 1996, published by Houghton Mifflin Company in Boston, Mass. ISBN# 0-395-69822-7, based on the life of Alton Lee Clement (Lee Nailling) an Orphan Train Rider to Texas in 1924. Warren wraps Lee's story around facts and background information about the Orphan Trains era in a way that is suitable for upper elementary students and adults. The book is sold by OTHSA and is available in many better retail book stores.

The Battered Child published in 1969 by Helfer and Kempel in Chicago, Illinois, gives an excellent background to the term "foundlings" and traces the care of "unwanted infants" back to the crusades. The book details the encouragement of Pope Innocent III (about 1200), for institutional care provided to foundlings in hopes of preventing infanticide.

Julius, the Street Boy by Horatio Alger (New York Trade Publishing Company, 1894) is a study of "street children" from personal experiences.

Growing up in old Kansas by Harry Colwell, autobiography, self-published.

Dangerous Classes and my Twenty Years of Work Among Them by Charles Loring Brace. Long out-of-print.

FICTION:

RODZINA by Karen Cushman is fiction but is among the most accurate accounts to be found. Published by Clarion Books in 2003, ISBN 0-618-13351-8, this book tells the story of an older orphan girl who is Polish. "Rodzina" means "family" in Polish. Cushman's story details the inward strength many Orphan Train Riders had to have to survive.

Joan Lowery Nixon and Jane Peart each authored a number of fiction books on the subject of Orphan Train Riders.

MAGAZINES;

Smithsonian magazine, August 1986/Donald Dale Jackson's article, *It took trains to put street kids on the right track out of the slums.*

First for Women magazine, 1991/Lisa Napell's article, *I Boarded the Train* on page 42. Interview with Alice Ayler, Orphan Train Rider.

Life Magazine, Spring 1900, special issue/Dennis Stinson's article, *Nobody's Children* on pages 80-81.

American History Illustrated, December 1983/Leslie Wheeler's article, *The Orphan Trains*

Reunions, the magazine, Autumn 1990, Spring 1991, Winter 1991

OTHER REFERENCES:

America 1917 by Rev. P. Blakely "A Heroine of Charity", story of Sr. Irene Fitzgibbons

American History Illustrated, Dec. 1983m oages 10-23

Benton County Dail Democrat [Arkansas] Dec. 20, 1987 pg. 7A

Catholic Charities by O'Grady

Catholic Child Care in the Nineteenth Century by Rev. O. P. Jacoby

Charleston Express [Arkansas] Feb. 4, 1988 "Orphan Train Rider"

Coffey County Today [Kansas] Jan. 20, 1988
DePage Progress [Illinois] Oct. 16, 1980, page 2A
Dependent Child by Thurston
Fifty Years of Charity, Golden Jubilee Booklet
Foundlings on the Frontier by A. Blake Brophy, 1972
Home Life in Germany by Charles Loring Brace, 1856
Homes of the Homeless Children, 1903 page 239
House of Refuge by Robert S. Pickett (Juvenile Reform 1815-
      1857)
Hutchison News [Kansas] Nov. 11, 1979 and Dec. 23, 1979
Kansas City Star [Missouri] Oct. 16, 1986 page 10
Lawrence Journal-World [Kansas] Mar. 27, 1988 Section C
Leslie's Illustrated Newspaper [New York City] Nov. 8, 1873
Life of Brace by Emma Brace
National Geographic Jan. 1988, page 30
New Orleans Medical and Surgical Journal June 1913
New York Daily Times [New York] Jan. 23, 1852
New York Daily Tribune [New York] Apr. 20, 1850, page 3 &
      May 2, 1850, page 3
New York Herald [New York] Aug. 17, 1896 (Death of Sr.
      Irene)
New York Times [New York] Sat., Aug. 15, 1896
New York World [New York] Aug. 17, 1896
Orphan Voyage by Ruthena Hill Kittson, 1965
Ozarks Mountaineer [Missouri] Jan-Feb 1987 pages 42-43
Public Charities (Catholic World) Vol. 17, 1873
Reminiscenses of Sister Irene by Eliza Ellen Starrs
Scholastic Scope Vol. 36, No. 12, Jan. 22, 1988
Smithsonian Aug. 1986, pgs. 95-103
Springdale News [Arkansas] Jan. 4, 1987, pg. 3A
St. Joseph Gazette [Missouri] Feb. 6, 1987 "Young at Heart"
St. Louis Dispatch [Missouri] Aug. 6, 1985 page 5A
St. Marys Star [Kansas] Jan. 26, 1988
Sunday Champion Jan. 22, 1937 "Sister Irene" by Marion
      Brunowe
The Charities Review II, Feb. 1893
The Children's Migration by Annette Riley Fry, 1974

The Cottonport Leader [Louisiana] Sept. 20, 1957
The Daily News [Galveston, Texas] Feb. 28, 1988
The Genealogical Helper Nov.-Dec. 1981, pages 7-9
The Hays Daily News [Kansas] Jan. 7, 1988
The Topeka Capital-Journal [Kansas] Jan. 10 & Feb. 25, 1988
The Wichita Eagle-Beacon [Kansas] Dec. 15, 19, 22, 1979
Times-Picayune [Louisiana] Oct. 19, 1975
Tulsa Tribune [Oklahoma] March 30, 1988
Tulsa World [Oklahoma] Jan. 16, 1988 Section A, page 10
Women's World July 15, 1986, pages 36-37

Guideposts March 1991 printed a story written about Lee Nailling, an Orphan Train Rider to Texas. In a section titled The Family Room, it stated:

Lee Nailling never saw his biological father again. The Naillings adopted him, however, and got permission to contact Gerald and Leo's adoptive parents. The three boys saw one another every summer. Lee's efforts to locate his brothers and his sister were unsuccessful until 1984. That's when stories about Lee ran in newspapers in both Vivian, Louisiana, and Watertown, New York. In May of that year the four surviving brothers were reunited in Texas. Gerald was killed in World War II and Lee's other brother and his sister also died. Lee's brothers surviving at the time were Ross Clement, Leo Rodgers and George Gildard. In 2004 they are all deceased. Gerald's military medals were donated to OTHSA for the Museum. He died aboard a Japanese prisoner ship when the American forces sunk the ship during the war.

Lee's story of finding his family as a direct result of newspaper articles proves how powerful the press can be in locating people both in this present era and long ago. Newspapers are one of the most valuable resources in pursuing family research.

RESEARCHING AN ORPHAN TRAIN RIDER

1.   If the person you are searching for lived after Social Security came into being (1936 or so) be sure to check the Social Security Death Index to locate a zip code where the last contact with the government came from. Using the zip code, you can find a town or area where the person was at and using the date you can possibly find an obituary. Sadly this does not work if you do not have their last known surname.

2.   Vital records prior to 1910 for the five boroughs of New York City are available at the Municipal Archives, telephone (212)788-8580 or write to:

Manuscript Archives
Department of Records
31 Chambers St., Room 103
New York, NY 10007
Go online at
http://www.nyc.gov/html/records/vitalrecords/birth.html

Department of Health has records after January 1, 1910.
Contact them at:
Department of Health
125 Worth St., CN 4 Room 133
New York, NY 10013-4090

For records outside New York City but within the State of New York, contact:
New York State Department of Health
Vital Records Division
Albany, NY 11237

Do not overlook probate records, will and deeds, plus marriage and divorce records when searching for information. Every public document is a possible source.

INDEX

Alger, Horatio	page 78
Ault, Jesse	page 48
Ayler, Alice	page 79
Beatty-Krout, Sheila	page 71
Bennett, Mrs. S. R. I.	pages 39, 40, 78
Blacklidge, J. C. & Mrs.	page 47
Blakely, Rev. P.	page 79
Brace, C. L.	page 27
Brace, Charles Loring	pages 11, 16, 26, 74, 77, 78, 80
Brace, Emma	pages 26, 80
Brace, J. P.	page 62
Brace, Rev. C. L.	page 14
Braly, Algie	page 6
Braly, Algier	page 4
Braly, Mr.	pages 3, 4
Brophy, A. Blake	pages 76, 80
Brunowe, Marion	page 80
Buckman, Marie	page 2
Burding, Wm. H.	page 47
Campbell, Helen	page 74
Cesqua, Mr.	page 21
Cheever, Mrs. George B.	page 14
Clark, Ira G.	page 47
Clement, Alton Lee	page 78
Clement, Gerald	page 81
Clement, Ross	page 81
Clore, Mrs. Mary	page 48
Coble, Janet	pages 36, 37, 69, 72
Colwell, Harry	page 78
Cooper, Rev.	page 47
Cooper, Rev. V. A.	page 46
Cooper, Supt.	page 48
Cooper, V. A.	page 50
Crenson, Matthew A.	page 35
Cummings, Rev.	page 47
Cummings, Rev. S. S.	page 46
Cushing, Miss Alice	pages 46, 47
Cushman, Karen	page 79
Darnall, J. M. & Mrs.	page 48
De Leleu, Maurice	page 28
Devlin, Mrs. Daniel	page 31
Donnelly, R. R.	page 44
Douglass, Frederick	page 9
Dunnaway, W. P. "Willie"	page 77
Edelstein, Joan	page 57
Edwards, Henry & Mrs.	page 47
Elwee, A. K. & Mrs.	page 47
Fairbanks, Nina	page 47

Ferguson, Doris	page 75
Fitzgibbon, Sr. Irene	page 79
Freeman, Dr. Ronald J.	page 35
Friedgen, Mr. H.	page 62
Friedman, Reena Sigman	page 53
Fruitnight, Dr. J. Henry	page 34
Fry, Annette Riley	pages 12, 72, 77, 80
Fry, C. R.	page 62
Fry, Charles R.	page 74
Gilard, George	page 81
Gillon, Edmund V., Jr.	page 75
Gottlieb, Martin	pages 31, 69, 75
Gould, Walter	pages 47, 48
Gourley, I. J.	page 62
Graham, Janet	page 27
Gray, Edward	page 27
Greeley, Horace	page 33
Guisinger, Mr.	page 3
Hanson, Mrs.	page 44
Harness, B. F. & Mrs.	page 48
Hockett, J. G. & Mrs.	page 47
Hodge, Robert	page 69
Holloran, Peter C.	pages 46, 52, 76
Holt, Dr. L. Emmett, Sr.	page 35
Holt, Marilyn Irvin	page 73
Howland, Dr. John	page 35
Huston, Thos. & Mrs.	page 47
Inskeep, Carolee R.	pages 68, 75
Jackson, Donald Dale	page 79
Jacoby, Rev. O. P.	page 79
Jenner, Mr. Solomon	page 36
Johnson, Mary Ellen	pages 6, 43
Keenan, Henry	page 48
Kellar, Miss Katie	page 48
Kildare, Margaret "Peg"	page 2
Kittson, Ruthena Hill	page 80
Knox, Thomas	page 32
Landon, George W. & Mrs.	page 48
Lanfear, Mrs. A.	page 69
Langsam, Miriam Z.	page 27
Lerner, Adele	page 24
Letchworth, William	page 53
Lincoln, Abraham	page 17
Littlefield, Holly	page 73
Lovejoy, Rev. Elijah	page 9
Lovjoy, Owen R.	page 76
Mack, G. E. & Mrs.	page 47
Madison, Charles A.	page 72
Magnusson, James	page 63

Marks, Frances   pages 63, 77
Mason, Hon. John L.   page 14
Matsall, Mr. G. W.   page 13
McBeth, Miles R. & Mrs. page 47
McCausland, Clare L.   page 44
McCrystal, Teresa Vincent page 31
McDonald, James   page 48
McEwan, Israel   page 69
McGowan, George & Mrs. pages 47, 48
McL, Dr. & Mrs.   page 47
Metcher, Charles   page 48
Minor, Mrs.   page 47
Minor, Mrs. C. H.   page 46
Mischler, Adam Lenard   page 3
Mischler, Barbara   page 3
Mischler, Elizabeth   page 3
Mischler, Fred   page 3
Mischler, Johnny   page 3
Mischler, Madeline   page 3
Morgan, Mr.   pages 3, 4
Morrison, Margaret   page 48
Morrison, Rachel   page 48
Nailling, Lee   pages 78, 81
Napell, Lisa   page 79
Nesbit, John & Mrs.   page 47
Nicholl, Dr. Mathias   page 35
Niles, Reg   page 24
Nixon, Joan Lowery   page 79
Northrup, Dr. W. P.   page 34
O'Conner, Mr. C.   page 20
O'Connor, C.   page 62
O'Connor, Stephen   page 77
O'Dwyer, Dr. J.   page 34
O'Toole, James M.   page 52
Palph, Harrold   page 47
Park, Dr. Edward R.   page 35
Patrick, Michael   page 77
Patterson, Charles A.   page 48
Peart, Jane   page 79
Pease, Mr.   page 14
Pease, Rev. Mr.   page 26
Petrie, Dorothea G.   page 63
Pickett, Robert S.   page 80
Pippert, Ben   page 63
Pope, Lena   page 47
Redmond, B. F. & Mrs.   page 48
Reiff, D. T. & Mrs.   page 48
Remer, Victor   page 69
Reynolds, Dr. J. B.   page 34

Riis, Jacob   pages 12, 15, 72
Riley, Tom   page 43
Ring, Mary G.   page 47
Rodgers, Leo   page 81
Roosevelt, President Franklin D.   page 28
Roosevelt, Theodore   page 17
Ross, Mr. John D.   page 36
Sanders, Ronald   page 75
Scott, Kenneth   page 57
Scribner, Charles   page 72
Sellers, W. P. & Mrs.   page 47
Sheehan, Rev. George   page 52
Sheets, Evelyn   page 77
Shipman, Dr. George Elias   page 32
Shultz, Christie   page 48
Shultz, George   page 48
Silver, Nathan   page 74
Skinner, J. W.   page 62
Smith, Delbert H.   page 47
Smith, Dr. J. Lewis   page 34
Smith, Elizabeth B.   page 47
Smith, Ida M.   page 47
Stanley, Wm. A. & Mrs.   page 47
Starrs, Eliza Ellen   page 80
Steele, Arthur   page 47
Steele, Charles J.   page 47
Steele, Jennie C.   page 47
Steele, Marion E.   page 47
Stewart, H. H. & Mrs.   page 47
Stinson, Dennis   page 79
Stoddard, Willard   page 48
Stygles, Herbert   page 48
Swan, Mr.   pages 3, 4
Tenopir, Mary   page 63
Tierney, Ann Alousia   page 31
Townsend, Mr.   page 62
Tracy, Mr.   page 20
Tracy, Mr. C. C.   pages 19, 62
Trickel, Evelyn   page 77
Trott, Mr. E.   page 62
Tucker, Rev. Elisha   page 44
Tyler, President   page 44
Van Ingren, Dr. Philip   page 35
Vignec, Dr. Alfred J.   pages 32, 35
Warren, Andrea   page 73
Watson, James & Mrs.   page 47
Wheeler, Leslie   page 79
Wheeler, Mrs. Charles Gilbert   page 44
Whitman, George A.   page 47

Williams, J. E.   page 14
Wood, Fernando   page 16
Woodward, Charlotte   page 6
Young, Patricia   pages 63, 77
Zigalotti, Bianca   page 68
Zimmer, Dagmar   page 74

About the Author:

Born in rural Madison County, Arkansas in 1939, Mary Ellen grew up in a family that valued relationships and family gatherings were common events. In 1956, Mary Ellen (Eubanks) married Leroy Johnson and their four children (Ben, Ron, Tony and Renee) were born in rapid succession. Being wife and mother became her desired career until the children grew up at the same time and left her with an "empty nest."

In 1986, Mary Ellen Johnson learned that a group of homeless children had arrived by train in her hometown in the early 1900's and were given to strangers. Why children had been brought from New York City to Springdale, Arkansas intrigued her so much that she began collecting their personal stories and, as a result, founded a not for profit organization, the Orphan Train Heritage Society of America, Inc.

In 2004, a celebration was held in Dowagiac, Michigan honoring the 150th anniversary of the first Orphan Train Riders and in October, 2004, the 75th anniversary of the last Orphan Train Riders was celebrated in Sulphur Springs, Texas. This ended her formal work of 18 years as "the Orphan Train Lady."

Teaching herself to use a computer, write a weekly column for a local newspaper, and to speak before civic groups; Mary Ellen began to gain confidence that a mother and grandmother could make a difference if the desire came from the heart.

Over the 18 years as Executive Director of OTHSA, Inc., Johnson helped compile five books on the lives of the Orphan Train Riders; hosted numerous reunions and corresponded with hundreds of surviving Orphan Train Riders. In addition, she wrote and edited a newsletter for the organization.

This work, *Waifs, Foundlings and Half-Orphans*, is an attempt to put on paper most of the research techniques she used over the years in helping descendant and Riders.

Oh, by the way, Johnson also writes children's stories and tells her grandchildren that she is the best Grandma in the world.

www.ingramcontent.com/pod-product-compliance
Lightning Source LLC
Chambersburg PA
CBHW060807110426
42739CB00032BA/3130

* 9 7 8 1 5 8 5 4 9 9 5 5 7 *